Eat Here

& Get Gas!

By

Charles M. Williams

© 2007 by Charles M. Williams.
All rights reserved.

No part of this book may be reproduced, stored in a retrieval system, or transmitted by any means, electronic, mechanical, photocopying, recording, or otherwise, without written permission from the author.

ISBN: 978-1-4107-6966-4 (sc)

This book is printed on acid free paper.

1stBooks – rev. 4/07/08

Thank You

Every time I open a book I notice those acknowledgements and I wonder, why do they always write a page or two thanking all these people that none of the readers know! It's sorta' like the newspaper one-line thank you I saw so many years ago in our local weekly: "Our sincere thanks go out to Willie Cobb for the Corn!" Something about that line has stuck with me for thirty years.

Now that I'm the one who has written this book I have a much better idea as to why people who write want to say thanks to special people, people like my wife Charlotte who has encouraged me in everything I've ever done. My boys for whom most of this was written (maybe help them figure who that masked man really was). Of course my own family, my sister Pat and Brother Verne, and my wonderful communities of Eastman, Chauncey, and Dodge County, Georgia, where all these stories took place.

I would like to offer a very special acknowledgement to the Stuckey's Corporation, Mr. Chip Rosencrans, the Stuckey family, and especially my friend and mentor, Mr. W.S. "Bill" Stuckey, Jr, for the cooperation, leadership and support to make this book a reality. I would encourage each reader to visit the Stuckey website at www.stuckeys.com and stop in all the Stuckey's stores across the USA to enjoy those famous "Fine Pecan Candies!" Stuckey's was an idea both ahead of and very much in tune with its times. In fact, it still is!

Can't stop saying thanks without mentioning my right arm and wonderful administrative assistant Dena Mullis for all her conscientious efforts and her hard work on this project.

One other person I want to be sure to recognize is Roseann Cordelli, a dear friend in Pennsylvania. Roseann put lots of volunteer hours and her amazing writing skills into editing and suggesting and helping me make this idea a reality.

What a fun project. I highly recommend it!

Introduction

Charles Williams' stories of growing up Southern are personal and insightful, hilarious and engaging. For years Charles has entertained countless audiences across the United States with his singing and comedy act. Now, with the publication of this delightful book, the wit and humor of Charles Williams is available to a wider audience, and it will be as treasured as an old friend – the kind of friend who is bright and observant, and whose storytelling powers always crack you up. The South is changing rapidly; "Eat Here and Get Gas" records what life was like in the fifties and sixties, and while that record will entertain the older generation with humorous reminiscences of a cherished past, the seriousness of this book as an historical record for future generations should not be overlooked. This book brought back wonderful memories for me, and it made me laugh. It would have done the same for my Dad. For my grandchildren, it will inspire them to respect the rich cultural heritage of those of us who were lucky enough to have been born Southern.

Billy

W. S. Stuckey, Jr.

Contents

Introduction v

"Yes, yes, Mawgritt, we really do wear shoes!" 1
Unusual Title 7
"Hey! How's Yo' Mommer' & 'Nem?" 15
MACS 19
What do you want…really? 27
Eat Here and Get Gas! 39
Land of Opportunity: GO-GO-GO 53
Trains & Eggs & OCS 67
A PhD from HKU 79
Something about Fans 91
Black Iron Skillet 97
It ain't wrong…Its jus' different! 105
Millionaire's Island 111
Ahab & Clyde 121
Little Jack 127
Night Riders 139
"Kennedy Half-Dollar!" 147
A Wing Tip Shoe 157

The Tooth-Dentist	165
Wakin' up is hard to do!	173
"What did the Preacher Preach about this mornin' son?"	181
Fire for Effect!	193
Just a simple, screened porch	201
Skelton Ears	207
"Wish I hadn't done that"	213
Field of Fire	217
Brother Dave	223
Do you choose to lift or lean?	229
Baby Elephants know	237
This ever-changing world	243
Hafta' sit on my hands	253
Where'd That Come From?	257
Amazing!	265
If not now, When?	269
$4,250.00 Turkey	277
Summary	289
About the Author	293

"Yes, yes, Mawgritt, we really do wear shoes!"

"If you ain't got somethin' nice to say about somebody, just don't say nothin!"
Vernon Williams

We hear it all the time, those same questions, those stereotypical groupings, those age old but strongly held opinions people who don't know the south seem to like to believe about us. For example: "Does anybody outside of Atlanta wear shoes?" Or, what about: "Do all southerners handle snakes in church?" And here's a perennial favorite: "Was anyone really "acting" on **Hee-Haw**?"

Just to set the record straight, there are lot's of people who don't wear shoes who live in the city of Atlanta. Some can't help it, some do it on purpose, and some just don't care, but I would bet there are some there and I would guess there were some in Philadelphia, Chicago, Los Angeles, and Seattle as well! Come to think of it, we were all barefooted before someone taught us to wear shoes in the first place! Besides, if you haven't felt cool, damp centipede grass on the bottom of your feet in the spring or summer, why, you could be missing yet another of life's most wonderful experiences. Go ahead! Park the wingtips! Shed the Hi-Heels! Scrap the pantyhose and get out there. You just might be surprised how southern we all are!

Did you know that the southern Diamond Backed Rattlesnakes "Rattle" to make sure <u>You</u> know where **THEY** are? It's one of those marvels of nature. That Rattle is a warning for you and me that danger exists, it is very close, and you and I should stop, visually locate, and hopefully avoid the danger.

Of course, there are people who "handle" snakes. Most of them do so for the purpose of extracting their unique venom. This dangerous process is necessary in producing an antidote for the unfortunate among us who either accidentally or purposefully ignore that deadly warning "alarm" and are in fact "bit" by a Diamondback rattlesnake. I salute these people. I have stood in awe watching and learning from some of them as they go about the business of educating and informing their audiences of the inherent dangers. I will always be amazed to see a man standing in the middle of a dozen or so *live* rattlesnakes, all of which are just a few feet from him, all arranged in a circle around him. It's all the more interesting that these dreaded, deadly creatures sit coiled,

Eat Here & Get Gas!

rattlers rattling, heads and eyes fixed on the professional following his every move, tongues sampling the air, and yet, never moving toward him.

Nature is amazing. These dangerous creatures sit, watch and rattle. In fact, if the professional takes a metal rod he would normally use to pick the snake up for whatever purpose, he can rub that rod back and forth, left and right, any which way touching the snake's head...and the snake will not strike at the object. Instead, he will just continue watching, rattling, and sampling the air with his forked tongue while he constantly keeps his eyes trained on the man.

Now, take a cigarette lighter. Heat that rod up, and then put it anywhere within the snake's striking distance of that snake's "nose" and he'll strike it again and again with lightening speed and deadly force. (Actually the distance varies with each snake but is generally determined by the length of the curve of his neck). You see, snakes aren't really "watching" but instead, they are sensing "heat", like body heat from a rabbit, a squirrel or other prey, or maybe the 98.6 degree temperature of a most unfortunate human being...and that's the signal that prompts the snake to strike.

Charles M. Williams

Knowledge is a wonderful thing isn't it? You have just learned that southern Diamond Back rattlesnakes will not naturally come toward you. They will give you every opportunity to stay clear by providing you a "warning" signal, that awful, terrifying, and very dangerous sound of their rattling tail. You have learned that their venom is necessary to create a medicine that is used to treat people who are struck, for whatever reason. Plus you have learned that there are people out there who willingly put themselves in grave danger to help create an antidote for rattlesnake victims.

Oh yes, there are people who believe handling snakes is a gift from God that proves something or another about their special faith or relationship to their heavenly father. The fact that these people might actually, physically, "handle" a snake and live to tell about it is amazing, but rest assured, it ain't all of us. I don't know the number or the percentage of churchgoers or any other "statistic" or where to find such numbers, but you can bet I ain't one of 'em. I don't even know one of 'em! I have been in church most of my life and I have never even seen one, other than on TV, and to tell you the truth, you and I both have seen raisins dance and sing on TV too, so, so much for that as a "proof" that something is for real or not!

Eat Here & Get Gas!

One other thought to ponder: No, I suppose everybody on Hee-Haw didn't have to act. Some were brilliantly talented. In fact some of the best guitarists in the world, people like Chet Atkins, Roy Clarke and so many other notables, Flatt & Scruggs...well, nobody in the world can compare...acting or not. The originators and producers of Hee-Haw correctly figured people everywhere had a stereo-typed image of "hillbillies" and "rednecks" and poked good natured fun at those groups with tremendous success. Sure, people in the south are different. We talk more slowly and we don't seem to be in quite the hurry our friends around the country seem to be, but you know what: Ain't so much difference from one corner of the US to any other! If you aren't sure you understand that fact pretty clearly, by all means, just pick any dictator in the world and ask him! I would be willing to bet they have figured out that even though there is incredible discontent, diversity, and differences of opinions about everything from automobiles to zoology, there is a brotherhood that exists under that ole' flag that is indeed a force to be reckoned with! Shoes or not, snakes or not, acting or not, I am very proud to be an American...and count it a special blessing to be southern!

Unusual Title

*Want a Success Formula? 10% Talent, 90% Discipline.
To succeed, son, persist!*
Vernon Williams

A journey of 10,000 miles begins with a single step. Chinese proverb. This writing is a collection of stories about the wonderful—if not original discovery—about how getting there is only the culmination of the journey. The fun is in the traveling. Another old Chinese proverb: "It's later than we all think…" that's why this project started!

Small-town Georgia has a very special place in my heart. It's what I know. It's how I grew up. It's my foundation and it's home after nearly five decades. "Eat Here and Get Gas" is my recollection of these brief years and the fun of living every day to enjoy the characters and the delightful humor that is everywhere.

If you can't find humor and a blessing in most things, what's the point? Laughter has healing power. There is actually scientific evidence that tells us about endorphins being released…those are chemicals that make your body feel better…and they come with an old fashioned belly laugh.

It is also ancient history–something people have known for a long, long time. Even in the Bible we find the concept: "A merry heart doeth good like medicine!"

There is indeed a healing power in humor and I believe, whatever political parties you belong to, whatever prejudices you have, whatever your socio-economic, religious, geographic or other boundaries you have, the joy of humor transcends them all and can help you feel better. Here's an example: I went to my doctor for an annual physical exam the other day. My doctor is a very knowledgeable and experienced physician, but he just doesn't share my sense of humor. Getting him to smile is a real challenge. It doesn't happen often!

Just before the physical, I got myself a pocket flask, like the ones people use to carry "wobble water" into football, stadiums...you know, they're flat and fit neatly into one's sport coat inside pocket. Can't you just see all these "alumni" flooding into the college football stadiums with five or six of these "hidden flasks" in their inside coat pockets? "Naw, man, I ain't got no liquor...!" Well, I filled my flask with apple juice and headed for Dr. Tison's office.

When I walked in, his nurse, my first cousin Carol who is also my wife's first cousin as well, go figure, handed me what she called a gown...you know, the little apron-like garment that ties twice in the back and gives a whole new meaning to the term, "I.C.U!"...and along with that "gown", I was handed a little clear plastic cup. I thought to myself, This ought to really be fun.

I stripped off naaked (genuine Southern term), filled up the little plastic cup from my little "UGA Flask" and went bopping down the hall to ask the nurses and Dr. Tison if they thought my cupful looked a little cloudy to them.

They said "Naw," but I went on to say, "Well, it looks a little cloudy to me, so I think I'll run it through again!" And with that, I turned up my little clear cup and drank it all down…while the nurses fainted and fell to the floor like two-by-fours dropped from six feet!

Just a little humor where you find it. You really can have great fun with the most common things and beleive me, it's all in how you see 'em!

For example, next time you're on an elevator, bend way over to a height-challenged individual and ask whether elevators smell different to short people.

While we're thinking about it, why is it that most adults seem to think good, clean fun is the province of young people only??

Well, back to the writing of "Eat Here and Get Gas!" This unusual title, like so much else in this old world, may not be what you think! The title comes from the story of my hometown, Eastman Georgia's most successful native son, and of course, the most financially-successful man I ever personally knew!

Charles M. Williams

This man sold rubber alligators, miniature bales of cotton, "Fine Pecan Candies", snack foods, and of course gasoline to Walter & Barb, Lucille & Rob, and all their fellow "Yankees" as they travelled south each year from Minn-SO'-Tuh and the other "snowbird" states on their way to Florida. It was a natural event every winter and spring extended to more and more people by the popularity of of automobile travel.

I have been to Minn-SO'-Tuh, friends, and from what I've seen, I can't blame anyone there for wanting to be in Florida in the winter! Nothing grows up there. The state tree is a telephone pole...and it was grown, processed, and hauled up from south Georgia!

I want to give you snapshot of childhood in the 1950s and 1960s in the rural Georgia South. I want to introduce you to some of my lifelong friends who continue to be my best memories. I'll tell you about some of the memorable experiences of growing up in the "boom" times of the post-war era. There are poignant stories of the characters who so shaped my earliest-and longest-held views of the world and there are things I ain't too proud of...but they're in here too.

I hope to share a laugh, put a smile on your face and share a few observations I have made in these first five decades.

Best of all, there is the thread of the joy of life, love, longevity, and family that I hope will help you realize, "It ain't *where* you are, it's *what* you are that counts!" And, to quote baseball great, Satchel Page: "Don't never look back...something may be gaining on you!"

One of my all-time favorite writers, Mark Twain, told this story about a young preacher in a revival service. Mr. Twain said the preacher was making an appeal for money. As most church-goers know, most any pew you sit in will have a card holder in front of you and the first two words will likely be "Welcome" and "GIVE", not unusual by any stretch of a Baptist imagination, and this particular preacher, Mr. Twain says, was emotionally involved. He made such a wonderful appeal that Mr. Twain thought to himself that he would give $50 when the offering plate came around. (*Quite a sum of money in those days*).

Twenty minutes later when the preacher was still going, Mr. Twain changed his mind and decided he would only give $25. Still another 15 minutes passed with the preacher still hard at it and Mr. Twain decided to cut his contribution down to five dollars.

Just over an hour later when the preacher finally quit and the offering plate passed in front of Mr. Twain, he said he took three dollars from plate!!

Unlike Mr. Twain's experience, I hope to keep you interested as you read these pages and make you glad you spent time here! If you have just half as much fun reading as I have had writing, we will both have had a wonderful experience!

One more thing: I have made the better part of my living over the past decade as a public speaker. I play a six-string Martin guitar, do a little finger-style pickin', add a little Southern talk about all sorts of subjects, tell a few jokes, sing a song or two, and I always come with a strong desire to help people by encouraging them to laugh a little. You know, turn loose, have a little fun. Fellow Georgian Ray Stevens' songs like MawGritt and the Mississippi Squirrel are always popular, along with Hank Williams, Don Williams, Tennessee Ernie Ford, John Denver...just a really positive program that people seem to enjoy.

I mention that to tell you my ultimate goal is encouragement- both in my speaking opportunities as well as through this writing endeavor. As you spend time here, look for the positives. Look for the humor. Look for the opportunities to laugh and smile. The difference in your life and the lives of those with whom you come into contact will be evident...and that, dear friends, is the reason for my effort! It ain't just the "getting there" that makes a journey worthwhile...*it's the traveling.*

Just one more thing: If you have a disagreement with somebody, doesn't matter if it's fresh or twenty years or more old, now, NOW is the time to clear it up.

Whatever it was about, who was right or wrong…it really doesn't matter. Chances are you don't remember most of the details anyway…and so what?

Worse yet, you probably never knew the other side of it in the first place.

Read this carefully:

***if you're still mad, you are very likely the only one who is** and guess what, your hate, disgust, dissatisfaction, and whatever else you might still be holding and feeling aren't affecting them anywhere close to as much as they are adversely affecting you!*

That case of gas you've been noticing for all this time, why, this just might be the cause. Ain't it time to let it go?

I think so, and I think you'll be all the better for it! Let'er roll boys! CMW

"Hey! How's Yo' Mommer' & 'Nem?"

"You can choose your friends but God gave you your kinfolks!"
Vernon Williams

That just about covers it all don't you think! The big, loud "HEY" is the attention getter. Follow that with a sincere question about the one person dearest to all Southerners, "How is your Mother?" or "Mommer as we say, and you have two of the three elements of the absolute, cover-everything-and-everybody greeting ever devised! The final segment is the catch all, strictly Southern version that includes dads, uncles, brothers, cousins, aunts, sister's, step chillen', somebody else's children, and folks who happen to be close for whatever reason…in fact everybody with the phrase, '& NEM!" Which of course means…and them…"all them other folks in the family!

Put it all together and it may well be just be THE perfect greeting:

"Hey, How's Yo' Mommer' & Nem!"

So let me ask you: *"Hey, how is yo Mommer' & Nem?"* See! Makes you feel good inside just to read it *"don't it?"* When you hear it in real life, in real time, by a genuine, sincere Southern friend or relative (and most all of us *IS* however distant) with a real live Southern accent, who is right there in front of you or on the other side of the country by phone...why it is a joy to behold! Just makes you feel like home! Makes your ears happy! Know what I mean?

Try it! "Hey! How's Yo' Mommer' & Nem?" Say it with en*THUS*iasm...you *will* be amazed. It is such a fine, cover-everything opening line, why, it could just become a prime part of your everyday conversations. It could become a theme you could use to start your days, you know, kick-start 'me and get 'em off to a higher level. Even more than you, your "hearers" will be amazed.

Fact is, it is comprehensive. If you say "Hey! How's you Mommer & 'Nem?", why, you have covered everybody and ain't left nobody out so won't nobody be offended. First, you used the proper Southern greeting: Not the Northern version that might say: "Geeze, Hello and how are you fine people this lovely morning!" Naw, just a simple HEY! Or maybe even a HEY YA'LL -if you want to spread it on thick.

Eat Here & Get Gas!

The, "How's Yo' Mommer…" part is best of all. Everybody with any kind of good raisin' in the world knows from the earliest age that "Mommer" is the most important living being anywhere and if "Mommer" ain't happy, why, it's true, ain't NOBODY happy…and here's one better, ain't nobody gonna' be happy either.

So, **HEY, HOW'S YO' MOMMER**…why, that's the proper greeting with the appropriate question tagged on right up front.

Try it next time you want to be clear and concise in your speaking:

"Hey! How's Your Mommer' & 'Nem?" Ya'll!
It just don't get no better than that!

MACS

The first step in getting where you want to go is figuring out where that is!
Vernon Williams

Marketing, Advertising, Consulting Services is quite a long name for a small business in the tiny town of Chauncey, Georgia. The beauty of MACS is that I heard most of the failure messages that, no doubt, you have too. But I didn't listen!

Fine, upstanding, well-meaning people hear about the idea you have for a new company and offer things like, "You're gonna do what?" "Start an advertising business? In Chauncey?" "Well, it won't work." "Ain't nobody never done that before!" "Why, you can't do that in Chauncey." "You have to be in a big city somewhere." "You're gonna fail!" "You had better keep your job as a loan officer in the bank!"

Ya'll, they're everywhere. Most of them mean well, and they really want to support you and your decisions. However, their message comes through loud and clear. You're the talk of the local beauty salon: "Did you hear that Charles is leaving the bank?"

"Why no, I hadn't heard that. Is there a problem?" *(Might be a bit of hope here for a juicy morsel of gossip. We love that in small towns you know).*

"Don't think so. But rumor has it he's starting a new business...something to do with advertising."

"You don't say. Is he moving to Atlanta? Are he and Charlotte having trouble? Is he running around?" Oh the rumors fly...

"Well, he oughta' stay with that good bank job. He's so nice to people. He is so good for the community. He ought not to leave that good, secure job to start no advertising business, whatever that is! And in Chauncey of all places! Well, I never! He ain't gonna make it. He'll be back in the bank. Just you mark my words. He'll be back!"

Rumors fly in small towns and I guess in larger ones, too. The tongues wag and the stories grow and grow 'til a change of occupation has you in all kinds of marital despair, health problems, and less-than-perfect performance records at your previous job. The creativity that goes into rumors surely could be more constructively harnessed elsewhere. Unfortunately, creativity is too often a wasted resource.

'Fact is, I am the same age as the guy who was my "boss" and very dear friend, Jim Williams, the bank president. He didn't plan to retire for many years and I figured I had risen about as far as I could in the bank. I believe I could have stayed. It felt pretty secure. It had a good future, but I believed there was something more out there for me to try.

The Stuckey family had purchased the bank from its long-time owners and one of my mentors in business, Mr. Welman McCranie. Bill Stuckey and his sister, Lynda Stuckey Franklin, are very good friends of mine and our family, and they are people whom I respect and admire. As the new owners, I figured I might have had an excellent future there. In addition, I loved the people I worked with and still feel a family closeness with them even though I have been away from the business since the late 80s.

Nevertheless, there was this burning thing down inside me telling me I had to see if I could meet the challenges of a new business venture. I had a unique opportunity and the time to pursue both my dream and my banking career, since our bank was closed every Wednesday. Our banking hours were like most small towns-open on Mondays and Tuesdays, closed Wednesdays all day, open Thursdays and Fridays and then open till noon on Saturdays. Employees were never more than two days from a day off. Still, I quit that job. Sometimes I still wonder about that!

Ain't no days off when you work for yourself, unless you look at work like I do. I love what I do so much that everyday it seems like a vacation! Working for yourself is really fun, but one big problem is that when I call in sick, I already know I'm lying!

When I worked at the bank, I spent Wednesdays traveling to nearby communities to talk about MACS *"Message On Hold"* telephone service, radio production capabilities, and graphic arts capabilities.

Selling is my thing. It's something that comes naturally. I enjoy it, and my efforts brought some early success. Of course, that led to buying more equipment, more supplies, and to building a small office and recording studio in my home. Charlotte got tired of me doing radio commercials at all hours in the house because it kept the boys awake at night!

Pretty soon a new building was constructed just away from the house. More equipment, more people and more customers, and MACS! soon became a little company with a pretty exciting future. We now serve customers in 15 states with various marketing, advertising, and training services and programs.

Somewhere along the line, my love for guitar picking and hearing people laugh created the opportunity for yet another career in entertaining groups of all shapes, forms, and descriptions. Who would have ever thought such an exciting future was out there back in the days of struggle with automobile floorplan interest rates of 21% and lagging car sales?

Eat Here & Get Gas!

'Fact is, <u>you have to be careful what you earnestly want and ask for in this life</u>! It is very likely to occur. All those years of listening to Ray Stevens and Jerry Clower recordings, Tennessee Ernie Ford's singing, Chet Atkins' guitar pickin and reading Lewis Grizzard books, didn't compare to seeing Brother Dave Gardner live in Daytona.

My sister took me. The man, Brother Dave himself showed up, in person, on stage, confederate flag vest and all. It was the early 1960's you know. When he finished telling his delightful story of the **"Origin of Rock and Roll,"** I knew I was hooked. Immediately, I knew I wanted to entertain. I wanted to do that kind of presentation in front of people. I had no idea how I could ever get there, but I had this wish, more like a craving, way down deep inside. The question was how do you do that from a place like Chauncey?

As the years have passed, MACS has become an excellent business. Harnessing the combined creativity of our writers, graphic designers, professional voices, sales and administrative people, our annual sales continue climbing year after year.

Billy Edenfield is an inspiration. This man has had the most serious health problems, surgeries, you name it. He has heart problems and complications, but, he doesn't roll over and give up. He comes in every day, makes calls, creates opportunities, and most of all, inspires all of us at Macs to ever greater heights. I don't think quit is in his vocabulary—and watching him, I know it can't be in mine!

Video production has added to our offering to make us a full service production company and our sales work in banks and other businesses has provided an extensive network of people who organize annual events. Guess who has been given the opportunity to speak, sing, tell jokes, and play guitar at these events? Can you imagine anyone who loves it better than me?

It just goes to prove, you gotta' be careful what you *really* spend your time thinking about, you know, what it is that you *really* want! You might just end up where I am now, combining all those wonderful memories into a life-long dream of managing a successful business that includes speaking and entertaining!

Now after more than 20 years of consistent work in marketing, advertising, video production, training for bank groups and classes around the country, endless hours of guitar picking, and hauling equipment into high school lunchrooms and Rotary Club ladies nights, I don't know anyone who enjoys the process more than I do. I don't measure success by bank accounts or national recognition but by the fun and pleasure my audiences and I get out of what I do. I would offer this advice from a lifetime of pursuing my

Eat Here & Get Gas!

"entertainment" career: You really should be careful what you wish for in this old world. It can happen. In fact, it does in many cases. It certainly has in mine!

What do you want…really?

"If you don't aim at nothin, that's most likely what you're gonna' hit"
Vernon Williams

"Oh you need to live in Atlanta." "You'll get used to the traffic." "You'll love the big city life." "With your talents in advertising and art, you NEED to live in Atlanta to be successful." "That's where the money is." "That's where you can get in touch with more people in your business, more contacts…"and on and on!

You know, <u>if you listen to other people and do what they tell you instead of listening to your own inner voice and your own common sense, you'll wind up somewhere other than where you really ought to be.</u> That's not meant to be profound. It's just a simple statement of fact. Aunt Julia, your friend, Bob, your barber, and the guy sitting next to you on an airline are all great people, no question about that. 'Fact is, they are not you. You are the only person out of all the billions and billions of people who have ever lived in this world who will ever have the opportunity to be YOU and get it right. PERIOD! End of statement.

The sooner you realize that fact and start down the trail that leads you to who you really are and who you really like being, the sooner you will achieve that proverbial state of happiness. Actually, you are already there; 'might just be a little cloudy between your ears yet!

'Fascinating thought. If you aren't completely sure of what you should be doing with your career, your long term plans, what you really want to do with yourself, regardless of age, maybe you can clear your foggy brain with the following simple exercise in imagination:

Just picture yourself, this instant, walking through this wonderful doorway, leading from where you currently are, into exactly where and what you would be if you could have whatever career you earnestly and deeply desire.

Of course, a rock musician on tour in Europe or a lottery winner spread out in silk sheets with a whole harem of beautiful, voluptuous, admiring women (if you're a guy with a wish or of course, the Chip'n Dale gang if you're a gal with a wish) those are fantasies. Those are not actual dreams like I would prefer you to consider.

For the majority of us, I am referring to a vision of that elusive career goal you've always wished for/dreamed about: Perhaps, trying a case in a court of law, practicing medicine, being a missionary in a foreign land (like California or maybe some even-stranger place in this world) entertaining people or groups, speaking, advertising, banking, military leadership, On and

Eat Here & Get Gas!

on and on your possibilities list can go, limited only by your truly-limitless imagination.

The one idea we're looking for in this scenario and mental exercise is whatever it is you **earnestly** desire to be, however far-fetched the concept might seem.

Now, for a few moments, forget any and all obstacles to your personal, deeply-held dream. Imagine yourself already having overcome those obstacles.

Whatever it is, you're there and you can actually "see" yourself doing whatever it is you deeply yearn for the opportunity to do. You are no longer involved in your current work-a-day situation, but you're over there, through the imaginary doorway to your ideal situation.

Forget the obstacles. Let them go for a moment. Of course you can overcome them for the purpose of this mental exercise. This is YOUR dream, remember!

Forget the difficulties! Disregard the *"trying-to-be-helpful"* voices of your mother, your barber, your co-workers, your best friends, and all those other people who will undoubtedly tell you dozens and dozens of reasons your dream won't work.

You realize of course these people are right! They are absolutely right, but **_only_** if you _**allow**_ them to be. Worse yet, if you let them, they'll prove it!

   You're the one who has to be convinced. You 'da man! You "Go Girl!" Even more importantly, you are the *only* one who can accomplish this task. Keep this thought in your head: before your dream *(or anything else for that matter)* can happen in this old world, it has to happen first in your mind. Get the picture! Get it clear. Get it down in your mind. That's what this exercise is all about.

   Once you firmly establish your goal in your mind, write it down. WRITE IT DOWN!

   This is the important part. Without a firm, solid, written-down-on-paper goal established in your mind, you are like a ship without a rudder: you have nothing to guide you to your logical conclusion. You are at the mercy of the wind and seas! However, with a goal so firmly established, you can move toward the objective…not without obstacles, but in spite of them…through them, under them toward, blast them out of the way and go on both to and even beyond your objectives.

   And get this, age doesn't matter. **Attitude does**.   Ability isn't the most important consideration. **Attitude is**. Talent is a wonderful attribute. **Attitude is incalculable**. Get the picture? Get the idea? **It's your attitude.** That is the most important thing.

Eat Here & Get Gas!

"If you think you are defeated, you are before you ever start." *(A quote from Henry Ford, my very first American icon).*

What is an obstacle? I believe an obstacle is that scary, ugly, treacherous thing you see when you take your mind and focus off your goal! Read that again! It might even be worth a yellow underline. An obstacle is the troll hiding under the bridge <u>between your present reality and your goals</u>! Don't look at the trolls under the bridge; keep your eyes focused on the goal way yonder on the other side.

Let's get back to the use of your imagination. When you have established the idea of exactly what it is you really want, step two is to determine exactly where you want to be.

I have been most fortunate in that I have had mentors throughout my life. People who cared enough to get involved, understand, and lead me to good decisions. Boyd Yarley was just that person at this juncture. His business sense, his keen understanding, his strong faith, and his leadership were crucial as I began to plan for the years ahead.

Mr. Boyd retired in the early eighties after having served as President of Blue Cross/Blue Shield of Georgia during it's start up and organizational phases. There are few men with a greater sense of business, technical operations, and marketing and promotion than Boyd Yarley. I will ever be indebted for his graciousness, kindness, and patience with me as Macs! came to life! In large part, the success of our company is based on the vision he helped us see.

<u>Find a mentor. Be a mentor.</u> The efforts are more than worthwhile and they are never forgotten. Answering the questions: What, where, when and how are much easier with the guidance of an experienced and capable mentor. I hope you can be so fortunate as I was to find Boyd Yarley!

My **"what"** was to be in the creative world of advertising. My **"where"** was our family home in middle Georgia. You can imagine the "That ain't gonna work" and the "It ain't never been done like that before" and the "You gonna "fail" messages I heard-again and again.

"Start an advertising company in Chauncey? Man, what's the matter with you? That won't work"…and so on and so on and so on. Aunt Julia, your friend, Bob, your barber, and the people you stand beside in the men's restrooms…all of them had a field day!

They were right, and if I had allowed them to, they would have proved it…just as they will do for you, but only if you let them. I decided against it! I decided this was my choice and not their choice…and MACS (Marketing Advertising Consulting Services) was born.

Eat Here & Get Gas!

After more than 12 years in business we're still growing and growing! How did that happen? Has it been easy? Have there been obstacles? Are there still? Oh man! Yes. Of course! But, don't you see? That's what a clearly defined, well thought out, written-down-on-paper goal is all about. When you take the time to think clearly enough to reduce your goals to written words on paper, something you will actually go back and read again and again, you have given your goals a life of their own. They are no longer simple thoughts floating around in your brain, they are concrete, tangible, living things! 'No longer abstract ideas, they are now benchmarks against which you can compare your efforts and measure your successes or failures!

It's a personal contract with yourself. A personal challenge. You aren't competing with other people or with the outside world any longer. You are competing only with what *you* believe you are capable of accomplishing. Writing your goals down is important. I hope you've gotten that idea!

Now answer the question, *what is **your** specific goal?* What have you written down? Why are you listening to all those well-meaning, but confused people? The choice, and that is what America is all about anyway, is your's—not their's—***YOUR'S!***

Whatever your present circumstances, they are in no small measure, the result of the choices you have made. (*Read that again and* *maybe even highlight it!)* If you are smoking dope-*you* made that decision. It was *your choice*. If you are an alcoholic-*you* made the choice. If you don't have enough money, think of the choices you have made that created this situation. If you consider yourself unqualified or not capable of something, that too is a **<u>choice</u>** you made.

The really good news is, that it isn't **where** you currently are that matters. The questions you need to ask have to do *first* with the choices you have already made that got you to where you are now, and next, and far more importantly, what choices are you going to make from this point? William James, the eminent psychologist, helped us discover that as human beings "we have the power to change ourselves by altering our thoughts and perceptions". It doesn't get any more powerful than that, friends.

Norman Cousins *"laughed his way back to physical health!"* What power does your perception and attitude have over your current situation? What about your future?

Mr. W.S. Stuckey, founder of the Stuckey's roadside store chain, could have easily chosen to find a job at some salary level and worked at that job throughout his career. Had he made that choice, few people would have ever heard of him. He could probably have supported his family and lived a good life, but his choice was to make incredibly-good candy and create a way to deliver

Eat Here & Get Gas!

that candy to customers! Great choice, don't you think? I hope you'll enjoy the story about him in a later chapter. He's another of my lifelong icons!

Fact is, your future is all about mental power! That power is at your fingertips right now, this minute, where you are this instant!

Henry Ford could have chosen to build his own "horseless carriage," the little four-spoked-wheel car he put together in his garage, and kept his little machine for his own personal use. No doubt, he would have been the envy of his neighbors. He could have remained "ahead of the Joneses" so to speak, but he made a different decision.

He chose to build cars inexpensively enough that many people could own and enjoy them. He didn't invent the car, just the process by which cars could be built and sold at a price that more than just the privileged few could afford! Great choice! That same power is available to you!

When you got up this morning, you had a choice. You either got up excited about the day ahead and about being positive with the people you might come into contact with today…or something less. Fact is, you made a choice. That choice was up to you. Nobody else! And by the way, ***if you got up on the "Wrong side of the bed", don't blame the bed!***

William James observed that we all have the ability…**all** of us…that includes me and you friends…to change our lives <u>simply by changing</u> our thoughts. Mr. Stuckey's thoughts were about putting a "sweet taste" in people's mouths. Mr. Ford's thoughts were about putting automobiles in the hands of people all across the country and all around the world.

Both of these men and all the rest of us saw obstacles to their dreams. Both of these men and all the rest of us have heard the well intended messages of our friends, families, and associates.

The difference is, these men established goals and kept themselves moving in the direction of their goals regardless of the messages and obstacles that came their way.

What about you? Are you moving purposefully toward your goals. Have you actually established and WRITTEN DOWN your specific, achievable goals…or are you still using your time, resources and energies reacting to the obstacles and messages that come your way?

It is a choice. It is **_your_** choice. Changing your life is a thought process which can be initiated right now, this instant! It is a decision you have to make.

In the end, your days are governed by the choices you make…step by step, day by day, choice by choice. Without a solid well defined goal, your choices will be at best, meandering. With your goal in mind, your path will be much more direct. The choice is yours.

Eat Here & Get Gas!

Just start with your imagination and let yourself go through that "imaginary door" to the job, career, profession, situation you would have if you could have anything you desired. Fact is, it's out there and by making the choices that lead to your written-down-on-paper goal, you **_can_** get there!

Mr. Stuckey did. Mr. Ford did. Charles is working toward it as you read this, and most importantly, **_(your name here)_** can too! Just be careful of what you really, deep down, with everything you got, wish for…you just might get it!

Eat Here and Get Gas!

"The Friendship of the Traveler means a great deal to us!"
W.S. Stuckey

Every morning started out the same. He made his rounds to the local farmers and landowners, buying all the fresh pecans he could. He wrote checks he only hoped he could beat to the banks. The farmers and landowners knew it was a race, and most would take their time getting to the bank with his checks...but some wouldn't. It was a race the man knew he had to win!

Of course, this wasn't just any man. This country boy was single-minded. Today, we'd call it "focused." He needed those pecans. They were his future. They were important. He could sense what was coming. He could see the future clearly enough to pursue his dream, regardless of obstacles!

Every day, Williamson Sylvester Stuckey left home early. He left his bride at home, busy over the stove, creating a concoction out of those pecans that would eventually lead to one of the great American success stories of the first half of the 20th century.

No matter! It was the stove, the ingredients, and the exacting old family recipes that were important. "Miss Ethel" was busy. (Just a side note here: Of course we all knew Mr. Stuckey's wife, Mrs. Ethel Mullis Stuckey, was a married woman and that her proper title was "Mrs.", however, in the Southern way, saying Miss for Ms., Mrs., and Miss was something we all did and indeed, still do! Thus, "Miss Ethel" was and is quite correct in this part of the world. 'Matter of fact, it goes with us where ever we go!)

In would come Stuckey, always in a slow, Southern hurry, to pick up the day's fresh concoctions, deliver the day's pecan purchases, and quickly depart to the Greyhound station, arms loaded with "Miss Ethel's" fresh "Divinity" for the travelers.

He had already worked out the original "sweet deal" with the bus drivers. "Let me on your bus for a few minutes while you load and unload packages and suitcases. I'll offer your passengers this wonderful Southern delicacy and to make it a 'Sweet Deal', I'll give you a package free, just for letting me on your bus!" he would say.

Today, there would likely be a federal investigation complete with special prosecutors, cameras, videographers, and a passel of reporters to "shed light on vice and corruption in the travel business."

But not then! It was business as usual in this small Georgia town in the mid 1930's. The unusual part was that this tall, delightfully-

Eat Here & Get Gas!

Southern talking businessman, was going about his work like a beaver building a dam.

The cycle was fast. The checks would sometimes "hit the bank" before the man could be there with the cash from the day's sales, and that could interrupt the steady flow of pecans to the kitchen, and so impede the next day's candy…it was a challenge! It was a fast pace. It was a cycle.

It was the steady rhythm, the very ebb and flow of life for this man and his wife and would have easily discouraged most people. But this wasn't most people. This was "Stuckey" himself. He could see what was coming! He believed in what he saw and he pursued his idea without regard to the cost or obstacles. He knew the "Snowbirds" travelled south each year in late fall. They were leaving the snow country headed for Florida (Northerners pronounce it "FLAIR'-ee-duh") Each spring, they would head back. It was a migratory event, as natural and certain as Canadian geese and winter itself.

He could see it coming and he wanted to be a part of it. He could see the obstacles, of course, but more important than those as facts, he could see them as stepping stones. He knew, instinctively, overcoming these obstacles would lead to his ultimate success. His attitude about that fact was more important than the fact.

Charles M. Williams

Greyhound buses, asphalt highways and eventually, automobiles and prosperity in the country were coming. They were coming fast.

It was a formula. A very successful formula for "Stuckey's!" The checks and the race and the challenge were merely obstacles to overcome, simply stepping stones.

Mr. Stuckey's engaging smile and slow, Southern style were contagious and unique. Especially with Walt and Barb and the snowbird gang.

The novelty of talking to someone who actually spoke not just Southern but smooth, precise, very positive Southern, excited people.

Mr. Stuckey had a gift of face-to-face communication. He had the ability to make you feel you were the most important person in the world and that you deserved and received his undivided attention. Your needs were paramount. Your friendship meant everything to him.

Can you recall how very special you feel when you are in the presence of someone with that very special ability? It is rare, and when you come face-to-face with it, the experience is one you won't soon forget! It is one of the many keys the most successful people seem to develop. Stuckey had that ability.

"Did you hear thay-at, Barb?" Walt might ask.

"Oh, jeeze yyyes. I sure dit! Isn't it just divine!?"

Eat Here & Get Gas!

"Delightful!" Walt would respond.
"Don't you think we should get some to carry home to Bill and Marge?"
"Oooh, of course"

And so the conversations would run in their Northern accents, all the while "Stuckey" at six foot two, would stand towering over the happy travelers entrancing them with his deep Southern accent, bright eyes, and charming Southern ways.

Just a side note here: Southerner's speak from way down inside and it's something Northern folks just can't easily imitate. An excellent example is the word H-E-R-E. A northerner trying to pronounce that word as a southerner would say, "HEE-YAA...".a sound not dissimilar to that of a donkey, "HEE YAHH" as Dan Acroyd did in <u>Driving Miss Daisy</u>." For example: "Moth-uah, I will put that over HEE YAA for you!"

A Southerner imitating a northerner with the same word would say something like, "EAR" from the high pitched back part of the throat "...come "EE' RR", this minute, you!!" (It just comes with the genes I think!)

Of course, all Southerners know instinctively that the word H-E-R-E is pronounced "eaah," like, "come eaah boy" or, "Look eaah son" or "Woah eaah, Mule!", but that's a whole 'nuther story.

"Stuckey" was, in fact, Mr. Williamson Sylvester, "W. S." Stuckey of Eastman, Georgia. He was named after H. G. Williamson, one of the original founders of Dodge County. There is an historic marble statue in the "Orphan's Cemetery" just north of town that marks Mr. Williamson's grave. This early settler was an orphan himself and donated the land for the now historic "Orphans" Cemetary, a regional landmark. Williamson was a very wealthy landowner in the earliest days of the 1800's and was an ancestor to "Williamson" Sylvester or W.S. "Stuckey".

The Stuckey name began to gain fame. Every Greyhound driver knew who Stuckey was and was glad to trade a few minutes of "aisle time" on his bus for the delicious candies "Stuckey" offered! It was a routine that was easy to get into. It was an original WIN-WIN-WIN situation. The drivers got their free Southern treat candies; the passengers got a close-up picture of "real Southerners," plus they got great candy they could eat or give as gifts to their families and friends. Mr. Stuckey, well, he got the money he needed to beat the checks to the banks. And he earned a handsome profit to boot!

Miss Ethel got the short end of the stick, to say the least. She got to stay in the kitchen and create sweet pecan candies for the next day's travelers. It was a very fast life in the slow, Southern style.

Profits were there and Stuckey (most of us were grown before we ever knew he even had another name) poured those profits back into his enterprise. More times than not, he beat the

Eat Here & Get Gas!

checks to the bank and was able to operate another day!

Profits and opportunities grew. Significant profits. In fact, they ranked right up there with huge opportunities, and Stuckey saw the future. He borrowed money and bought a small piece of land just south of Eastman on highway 341/23, the major thoroughfare of the day for travelers headed south toward "FLAIR'-ee-duh." He built his very first store and convinced the bus drivers to stop by as they headed south and to let the passengers have a few minutes to walk around, eat a snack, look at souvenirs, and of course, buy candy. Naturally, the drivers got free candy or a free lunch or just about anything they wanted because they controlled the customers to Stuckey's new store…and they were important. Mr. Stuckey not only knew these drivers were important, he made them FEEL important. No doubt this was a solid foundational block to his eventual success. You better believe if a driver had a choice of stopping at a typical filling station where he almost felt he was an inconvenience to the station management, or stopping at Stuckey's where he was made to feel like he was "King of the Road," he planned his trips to stop at Stuckey's! Fact is, that trend continued for more than 50 years as buses and automobiles from all over the country made a point to stop at Stuckey stores along the nation's most-traveled highways in or near more than 400 Stuckey's communities all across the USA!

The lesson is simple: If you treat people well, they'll treat you well! It's Biblical, you know. "Do unto others..." It's just that Stuckey had a natural flair for this kind of thing. He made everybody feel important. **_His philosophy for opening stores was based on the idea that if he could help enough other people get what they wanted, he would be able to get what he wanted at the same time!_**

Here's an example, not from a textbook or from some library research; it's from the school of "Hard Knocks," otherwise known as HKU, the University some of this country's most successful people graduated from...with honors! When Stuckey found what he considered an excellent location for a new store, which was practically every location at the time, he called on his friends and associates around home to tell them where he was thinking about building.

He told them how much it would cost for them to buy the land and build the new store on the site he had selected. He wanted them to make the investment based on his knowledge and track record. His part of the deal came from the exclusive candy, gasoline, and novelty sales. He knew if they were successful, he would be successful. They all knew travelers were

Eat Here & Get Gas!

comfortable with Stuckey's. After all, it was the original roadside stop.

Stuckey's had clean restrooms! Up north, gas stations advertised "Sparkling Restrooms!' while down South we advertised "Stuckey's PEE-CANS" *(early Stuckey's joke).*

There were all kinds of novelties for people to browse through and buy, buy, buy! Can you imagine Walter and Barb loading up a sack-full of rubber alligators on their way back to MINN-SO tahh and the joy on their kids' faces when they got those things to play with in the car? (There were no video games in those days. In fact, the first "record players" in cars which came with Disney's original "Davey, Davey Crocket" record that skipped and skipped with every bump, and even that didn't come along until years later.)

And what about Gramps and Gramma when they got those delicious Southern "Fine Pecan Candies" as a gift from their children just back from "FLAIR'-ee-duh?" Sheer joy and happiness. Who cared about calories?

It was indeed a highly-successful formula and one that worked flawlessly and quite successfully for nearly 50 years. It was long before McDonald's or convenience stores, or shopping centers or air travel or most any of the things we know and take for granted today.

In the beginning of cross country family travel in privately owned personal vehicles, there was

Stuckey's and you could stop there to take a break, shop a few minutes, use a restroom, enjoy air conditioning in the store 'cause cars didn't have it...hadn't even thought of it in those years! You could eat a snack or a meal, buy candy, and of course, get gasoline. The phrase "Eat Here and Get Gas!" is in there somewhere, but like most things in this old world, it's probably not what you expected.

The Stuckey success story is an icon for me. It is a powerful, motivational story. Here was one man in a tiny, rural community. Not a big-city high roller, but one man whose idea of high rolling was giving a a fifteen dollar check for pecans and working like the devil to beat that check to the bank. It's a story of taking an idea and turning it into a very successful business enterprise.

In the 1960s when the Pet Milk Corporation bought Stuckey's, something on the order of more than twenty million dollars was paid to Stuckey in cash and Pet stock. Not bad for a guy who started out beating checks to the bank! Don't you think?

Even better, his idea of success was measured not by how much he accumulated but how well his friends and business associates did! Don't misunderstand. It wasn't all peaches and cream, but the fact is, when Stuckey died in 1977, (same year as Elvis) Paul Harvey made the comment that there were more millionaires per capita in little Eastman, Georgia than in any other place in the

Eat Here & Get Gas!

world, of course, a direct result of the very successful and nationally-recognized Stuckey's operations.

That's a pretty impressive legacy and that's the icon of Stuckey's. In the words of one of America's wisest investors, "You can get anything in this world you want if you'll help enough other people get what they want." Mr. Stuckey sure did! So have the most successful people in America!

There is a lesson here for all of us whether in business, family, social relationships, marriage—practically any situation—helping other people results in good things happening for you!

Eat Here and Get Gas is, in this light, all about the basics. It's about achieving success by establishing and focusing on your goals, believing in yourself, helping others, having fun, and of course hard work.

It ain't *where* you are but *what* you are that counts. That's important! Go ahead, use your highlighter here so you'll notice this point when you come back and try to find a few good things from these pages.

One of my fondest personal memories of Stuckey is of my 5th birthday. Stuckey and my dad were good friends. In fact, Stuckey always wanted to buy my dad's house, and did once, but my dad wound up asking to back out of the deal when my mom couldn't bear the thought of never coming back there.

Charles M. Williams

Back to the birthday party. I remember playing in a little wading pool just outside the living room at our home. Stuckey was inside talking with my dad, Vernon. I was oblivious! Just then, the door opened and out came Stuckey and my dad!

Apparently, my dad had told Stuckey it was my fifth birthday, and this really tall (particularly to a 5-year old sitting in a wading pool) man gingerly bent down and handed me *five dollars* as a fifth birthday present. This was 1956 remember.

Regardless what Mr. Stuckey ever did, how much money he made, how famous he ever was or ever would be, I knew this was a very special man. He had done for me what he did for many other people…he had made me RICH beyond my wildest imagination.

I never forgot.

Eat Here & Get Gas!

Land of Opportunity: GO-GO-GO

The only place you'll find success before work is in the dictionary!
Vernon Williams

It was 1916 when my daddy, Vernon Williams, was born in rural Emanuel County, Georgia.

Vernon was the second of five children of J. R. and Molly Hicks Williams, and he arrived at a time when America wasn't the wonderfully prosperous country many of us have enjoyed in more recent times. Very likely, many of us find it hard to believe it was ever anything else.

Vernon knew. His leg was broken in a wagon accident on the way to town when he was a child and it was apparently set incorrectly.

For the next 40 years it was an obstacle. A big obstacle. Much bigger in fact than most people could handle.

Funny thing about obstacles though: they're what you see when you take your eyes off your goals—and Vernon Williams had an uncanny ability to focus on what he considered important.

His tremendous success in his very short life is a clear testament to his abilities.

Charles M. Williams

Operations, pain medicines, specialists and procedures were the order of the day throughout his life, all to little avail. The primary result of all his surgeries created a rather unnatural limp, a most unnatural walk that I copied, if subconsciously, and carry even to this day.

I deeply admired this man and wanted so badly to be just like him, Camel cigarettes and all!

His parents were sharecroppers. J.R. was a bright and capable man and he wanted little more than to bring his own family out of the struggle and financial strain of the times and like many others, he moved in search of better circumstances.

Eastman, Georgia was a relatively prosperous community back then. It was a railroad town with thriving agricultural, timber, and commercial enterprises. J.R. moved his little family away from their existence as farm hands, sharing their labor for a part of the crop.

He went to work in the ice plant in Eastman, delivering ice to home after home for use in the ice boxes- the forerunners to today's refrigerators.

People liked his personality. He was smart. He worked hard. He was careful with his money. He made friends and kept his eyes open for opportunity.

Until his death in 1957, J. R. bought and sold houses, cars, and machinery of all types and descriptions. At the same time, he continued his job in the ice plant, at least and until refrigerators

Eat Here & Get Gas!

came along and eliminated the demand for ice, and consequently, his job.

I can vividly remember his long index finger dipping into his tea glass on Sunday to swirl the ice in his glass during the Sunday dinner prayer. (*His index finger was longer and much bigger around than the other fingers of his hand. Under different financial circumstances he might have qualified as a fine doctor. Ponder that friends, but that's another story.*) Miss Molly wasn't impressed with J.R.'s stirring during the prayer, but we grandchildren loved it!

Dad's oldest brother was I. J. I'm really not sure where the use of "J.R." and "I.J." came from or if there is any significance to the use of initials instead of proper names in the Williams family. Could be just be a happy coincidence.

At any rate, I.J. could remember every single tag number for every car in the county. That was quite a feat of memory and old family friends remark about it even now, more than 60 years later. I.J. was a pilot in World War II and never came home from Guadalcanal. Miss Molly and J.R. never got over their loss.

Vernon was left the last and oldest son with three younger sisters-Minnie, Sue, and Margie. His mother, Miss Molly, died with cancer in 1959. I was almost 8.

Vernon was resourceful. I guess it was partly from necessity and partly from pure ability. He was likeable and bright and he loved the business of selling. He wasn't a HIGH PRESSURE sales type, but a man people trusted.

They brought him their needs and questions and he could always find products, in this case cars or repairs, to help them meet their needs and solve their problems.

There is a lifelong lesson here: something about helping enough other people get what they want resulting in you to getting the things you want. Vernon Williams might never have put that thought into words or sentences, but the fact that he put it into practice is clear!

His earliest job was in the Eastman Cotton Mill where he limped to work about 4 a.m. each day to pull an eight to ten hour shift. He earned a fair wage for his labor but most of all he got to know the people he worked with.

Afternoons were spent buying old cars and shaping them up to resell to those same folks. It was an enjoyable habit. His "customers" were his friends and fellow workers and they thought of him as someone who was helping them get something they wanted at a fair price. He prospered with this "sideline" for years before he eventually left the mill and began working for the local car dealers. He never forgot the concept of helping friends and neighbors achieve their goals.

By the late 1940's, WWII had ended and prosperity was on the horizon. Everything was

Eat Here & Get Gas!

scarce from tires to parts and, of course automobiles. The demand was great and increasing, which was opportunity knocking for this slightly-crippled salesman. He took advantage of his opportunities. He traveled anywhere to find cars and brought them back home to sell to his friends and neighbors.

Success came, but not without lots of hard work and effort and not without obstacle after obstacle. I can remember him telling me, "Son, the only place success comes before work is in the dictionary!" Mr. Stuckey was rich. I knew that. The Rockerfellers were wealthy. The Fords were known around the world, but none of them came close to my dad in my eyes. His simple philosophy and his HKU education placed him above the ranks of all the rest!

He married into one of those sad, but truly classic American situations. The girl he loved was a black haired-beauty whose mother didn't think the son of a sharecropper (or anyone else for that matter) was good enough for her daughter. His mother-in-law would not agree for her daughter to see this young man. But as fate would have it, they secretly met and were married almost a year before other people were told, especially her mother! 'Sounds familiar doesn't it? Shakespeare recognized the problem, the futility and madness of it in <u>Romeo and Juliet</u>. Needless to say, it has been around a long time and will likely continue!

Usually after the initial shock of such an event, everyone settles down to the facts and moves on with life, but Vernon had a formidable adversary in his mother-in-law. He *never* measured up, even though he supported her financially, allowed her to live in his own house, and even took her along on family vacations.

She outlived him by almost a decade and never changed her thinking. That he could just live with her constant disdain was heroic. That he went on to be a successful businessman in spite of it was incredible. That he died at 54 might have been anticipated. His short life was filled with work, pleasure, and a generosity that will be remembered long years from now.

My goals in life were firmly established from observing him. I think about how he did things and how he would do things if he were here. He was an encourager and I have tried to emulate that quality! He knew, instinctively, how to **"get up and get at it"** everyday!

He set goals and worked with precise focus toward achieving them. All of us were born into the land of opportunity by the grace of God! My dad knew how to take that privilege and parlay it into his personal, specific plans. The concept: **GO-GO-GO** is a picture of him in action!

I was born in 1951, at the beginning of a wave of prosperity in our country unlike anything that had ever come before. The war was over, the

Eat Here & Get Gas!

baby-boom generation was toddling about, and America was booming. Transistor radios were just ahead, "Etch-a-sketch." was the toy to have, and you were the kid everyone envied if you had a trampoline.

Our 300 acres were just north of the city of Eastman the town where my dad's Ford dealership was located. Right in the middle of our land was a beautiful pond he built, and behind it was a huge, long, green brick home that, at the time, had an unheard of convenience. Something brand new to the late 50's, central air-conditioning.

My mother always drove a brand-new "T" Bird. My brother had jeeps of every shape and description. My sister had a car when she was only a youngster (she could only drive it on the farm, of course…of course!) and I had a little gasoline engine "Model T" Ford!

We were in "High cotton"–a good Southern term which means about the same as "sittin' pretty!" and "High on the Hog!"

I thought we were among the wealthiest people anywhere and I actually thought we were related to the Henry Ford family! We lived like millionaires. Every summer we spent a month or two at our home in Daytona Beach. With a birthday on July 6th, I always believed the fireworks and celebrations in Daytona and everywhere else were for me! My brother and I had new Schwinn Corvette bicycles, Honda and Harley motorcycles, new clothes, and new cars and everything else you could imagine.

From my perspective, we were very well-off. My entire world existed between Route 2, Cochran Road, that long green house in the pines behind the pond, and Dodge County Motor Company, my dad's Ford Dealership and dream in Eastman.

I hardly knew there was a world beyond all that. 'Didn't need to. 'Didn't want to. 'Wasn't much interested. We had so much I was always just a little embarrassed. My life was pretty well established from my youngest days. I just knew I would finish high school, marry, and run the "Ford Place!" Mr. Stuckey was a personal friend of my daddy's, and me too, of course. He did give me 5 dollars on my 5th birthday you know.

Following my life-long outline, I finished high school in 1969, made a wedding date for June 1970, and was all set.

America put a man on the moon that very year. How could things have been anything but superb? It was great! My mother wasn't at all pleased to learn I gave my long-time girlfriend an engagement ring, sounds familiar enough doesn't it? She didn't speak to me for a week and a half that year, including my birthday, but no matter. All was well from my perspective. You know, **GO-GO-GO!** Like father like son.

The news from Vietnam was somewhat troubling, however. Something about a "TET

Eat Here & Get Gas!

offensive." I thought the National Guard was a safer plan and got my name on the waiting list.

In January 1970, I was off to Fort Polk, Louisiana for basic training in an infantry company. There were so many people at the induction center, 25 Greyhound buses transported hundreds of us up to the snow and ice country of Fort Campbell, Kentucky. It was winter, it was cold, it was depressing. Basic military training isn't a particularly enjoyable experience anyway, but even less so in snow and ice. Particularly if you came from a place where cold weather just didn't happen! Here I was, a "silver spoon and all" from a well-to-do family subjected to these fundamental and almost boring procedures.

Suck-it-up and go, it'll be over in May, I thought, and then it's back to the real world, GO-GO-GO, you know!

Just a few months, and everything would be back to normal, just like always. And best if all, no Vietnam! Make the best of a bad situation!

Our group completed BASIC training and shipped back down to Fort Polk for "Advanced Individual Training." It was the home stretch. I knew I could "hang by my fingernails" from here. Go-GO-GO!. *"Two more months and we'd be through...I'll be glad and so will you"* the marching cadence went! Warmer weather, no more snow! Things were looking up!

As so often is the case, things changed abruptly. Life has a way of doing that, you know. On Sunday night March 30th, I was awakened around 1 a.m. and told my had dad died earlier in the evening, the result of a massive heart attack.

I always will regret the simple fact that I never got to know him as an adult. That was a very challenging and difficult time in my life and remains a point of deep meditation for me even after more than 30 years. The most important and lasting memory that I have is that he knew me and actually liked what he saw.

Can you imagine what a valuable image it is and has been for me to have that fact in my mind all these years?

It was, and is, an indelible image. Even though he was very busy, very successful, and very involved in his work and community, he found a way to make sure I knew he not only loved me as his son but that he liked me as a person. He left me with the confidence that I could accomplish just about anything I set my mind to and that I could find a solution to just about any problem. When you get right down to it, there's not much more any kid could ask from his or her dad. Mine came through with flying colors! If I learned anything at all from him it was to make absolutely certain my children would grow up with that same wonderful, no strings attached confidence he gave me. It has lasted to this day and has, I hope and pray, been passed along to my sons!

There was a long wait to get home. There was the funeral, my family, and business to attend to along with the impending purchase of a house in Daytona that needed to be completed. And all in a little less than a week on leave from training in Louisiana.

I got a Red Cross extension for a few days through the efforts of a very dear friend, Mr. Buford Revel. I did what I could at home and returned to Fort Polk to find things had changed there as well.

At home, people were very kind and said nice things to me about my dad. "Charles, so sorry to hear about Mr. Vernon...what a fine man...and other such pleasantries as you might expect in a small community during such a terrible experience.

At Fort Polk, Sgt. Eason was something less than kind and informed me I would be "Recycled!" Nowadays, that's a good word 'cause it means using aluminum and glass again and again. But on that particular day, it was not a good word 'cause it meant repeating weeks and weeks of training and that meant weeks and weeks added to the time before I could go home.

Things had changed in a big way! As had always been the case with my dad, that change was actually the proverbial "Knock on the Door!"

I didn't recognize it as such until years later, but just as he had done all his life, I had come upon a major obstacle…and I was about to see if I had what it took to turn it into an opportunity!

I had learned about an OCS (Officer Candidate School) starting that May. Before this situation occurred, I hardly knew what OCS was and certainly had no intention of going through it. I just wasn't interested. Wanted to serve my country through the National Guard, participate in weekend assemblies, go to Fort Stewart in the summer for a couple of weeks, and hopefully, get out when my time was up! Lot's of young men had that same idea in those years: Serve your country but stay out of Viet Nam.

However, with the changes I was experiencing at that moment, I realized that starting OCS in May meant I had to finish Advanced Individual Training ("A.I.T."..the army likes to use acronyms even though spelling that word would prove challenging-to-impossible for many of the people who revel in using them) at my previously-scheduled time!

Friends back home pulled the right strings and an OCS acceptance letter was received by my training company commander out in Louisiana. He gave orders to my company first Sergeant ``to get me caught up and finished with the course on my original schedule

By that time, I was already weeks behind and decidedly not one of the good Sergeant's favorite trainees. Needless to say, it was a challenging six-week period and when I completed the training cycle on schedule, I was able to "max" every part of the physical training requirements.

I was quite ready for OCS.

Things were looking up again. Perseverance was paying off: Always has, always does, always will. A new opportunity was at hand and it would lead to absolutely incredible friendships and possibilities—at the time unimaginable but, as the years have proven, unmistakable.

My job, like my dad's before me, was to see the obstacle, turn it into an opportunity and **GO-GO-GO!** That's just what I did.

Charles M. Williams

Trains & Eggs & OCS

People are about the same everywhere. That's life. How you perceive those people, well, that's Your life! Attitude is everything.
Billy Steele

Among my earliest mentors is my old friend, Billy Steele. He lived then, and still lives to this day, in his old home place about half a mile back toward town from our house.

Just two houses further toward town than Miss Irene from our house! That's the way you give directions in places like where we live in rural Georgia. Ain't much need for street names and numbers here!

To say Billy was an unusual or eccentric character doesn't begin to describe him. He still has the huge stuffed rabbit *(outfitted in formal pastel attire no less)* he played with as a kid.

Now, 60 years later, and he still had an antique Buick "Limited" four-hole limousine built back in the mid 1930s. He kept that beautiful automobile up until 1980 when he finally got married.

The most amazing thing about this great big man was his love for trains. No doubt, he was a frustrated railroad engineer. He still has a very complex, working rail yard in what was once, a garage on the back of his house.

Charles M. Williams

Steam engines, freight trains, passenger trains, scenery, working bridges, storage buildings...intricate detail and painstaking work are evident in every square inch of this very large display. His invested hours of tender loving train care are incalculable.

To say Billy was meticulous and methodical is an understatement. To say that I was fascinated by his huge investment of time and money in this train display is also an understatement, however, my fascination was two fold. First, I wondered why a grown man spent so much time with model railroad buildings and trains. I was just a kid you know. Secondly, my imagination conjured up all sorts of possibilities for creating genuine havoc: wonderfully destructive things like collisions, bridge removals, M-80 explosions, and all sorts and kinds of mayhem.

Can you even begin to imagine the pleasure my friends and I might have had if Billy had not been ever on his guard!

Of course, Billy was acutely aware of my imagination and was beyond careful to keep me at bay most of the time. In fact, I think he could see the glow in my eyes as I stood up on tip-toes to see the mighty engines at work in his marvelous miniature train world.

As a young man, among other things, Billy sold eggs. He had chicken houses behind his house, and he gathered the eggs and sold them to his

Eat Here & Get Gas!

neighbors out on the Cochran highway and beyond.

However, it wasn't the sale of eggs he sought with his business venture, but much more, the opportunity to sit and talk with customers who so inspired him.

Fact is, I believe he would have given the eggs away, he mostly did anyway, just for the opportunity to sit and talk with people. Taking the time to become genuinely interested in people invariably resulted in having them become interested in him and I believe that was his inspiration to learn all he could about other people. **'Excellent goal by the way!**

That intense interest has served him well through his life and has helped him rise to unanticipated heights of success physically, financially, as well as in his church, his marriage, his family, his community, and his career.

I can remember his parents, Inez and Aubie Lee, or "Aubie" as most folks knew him. She was a school teacher who was well respected. He was a retired rural mail carrier and a prize fighter, and had been known to jog all the way to the next town, 20 miles away to the north, shadow boxing all the way there and back. Physically fit at all times.

Billy was an only child…We really should be thankful for small favors! He and his oversized stuffed rabbit spent quite a bit of time together.

Fact is, I bet they still talk from time to time, the rabbit being the consummate listener, and of course, that's what Billy really prefers anyhow!

Billy could sit and talk literally for hours, hardly ever mentioning eggs but always, and with significant, colorful if one-sided detail, describing the villagers.

Billy Steele was obsessed with the villagers, the individuals who made up our little community. He knew everything about all of them. What they did, what they should have done, why they didn't, and why he wasn't terribly impressed. Without notice he could be counted upon to fervently admonish the locals, all sorts of vice and folly with an edge that elevated satire to an art form.

From his front porch, his rocking chairs, and his stout beer in a frosted mug, four ice cubes and a dash of salt, toasting equally the passing natives and tourists. All sorts of wisdom spewed forth, and to a young highly-impressionable mind, it was a heady time.

Billy was a trusted friend and confidant. He had a good grasp of the overall picture and could readily fill in the details with his own vivid imagination and would happily do so, whatever the subject at hand.

He was long in wind, short in fuse and ever the procrastinator in marriage. The meticulous, old-fashioned, stubborn, only child, and confirmed bachelor raised in the era and shadow of World

Eat Here & Get Gas!

War II and trained to be several steps to the right of conservative was my first exposure to the word "eccentric."

And even if it isn't the precisely correct word to describe this individual, it's about as close as there is without creating a new one! How many 50 year olds do you know who have never married, have horse-sized dogs in their homes, peacocks out back (King Solomon had those) and more than 500 square feet of highly detailed and excessively expensive working scale model railroad displays as a part of their homes?

To say the least, my friend Billy Steele is a memorable character, a villager of the first order.

Billy was there in my earliest recollections and played a particularly significant role in the most difficult time of my life, mentioned in the previous chapter—just after I lost my dad in 1970.

I was 18. The youngest in my family, I was at that particular time, a military trainee about three weeks into training cycle stationed at Fort Polk, Louisiana. Billy had been a National Guard Officer for many years at this time and was a Captain with an unusual, even obscure though quite well connected unit–who could've expected less!

It was Billy who encouraged me to consider Officer Candidate School, (OCS) upon the completion of my training and, as it turned out, the next Georgia Military Institute OCS program would begin immediately after my training cycle was completed in Louisiana.

I considered the possibilities and basically dismissed the idea until after I had actually arrived back in Louisiana after my dad's funeral and found myself "recycled" into the next training group.

It was my time spent with Billy over the years prior to my dad's death and on the three-hour trip back to the Atlanta airport with him (don't all trips begin and end or at least at some point pass through the Atlanta airport?) after the funeral that would indeed change my life forever.

I called Billy, or then Captain Steele, who called his very good friend and soon to become my very best friend, George, or then Captain Hearn, the assistant commandant of GMI. Strings were pulled (snatched, jerked, and cajoled actually), orders issued and, one week later, I was accepted into the GMI OCS program that was to begin June 7th a very significant date.

To meet that date, meant I had to be through with the training in Louisiana. The good news was, not only could I **_not_** be recycled, but in fact I **_had_** to be caught up with my original cycle (I was three weeks behind at this point) and complete the course at my regularly scheduled time!

My friend Billy had come through with flying colors! He had turned a crushing loss in my father's death further complicated by a very difficult challenge to the military bureaucracy, into

Eat Here & Get Gas!

a positive situation. **GO-GO-GO!** That, friends, is what friends are for. All I had to do was go through OCS at GMI under George Justus Hearn, III. How tough could that be?

Having just read former Georgia Governor Zell Miller's book, "Corps Values," I can readily identify with the fundamental principles he covers with much respect.

At GMI, George Hearn was the Marine Corps, the Army Air Corps, the Navy, the Coast Guard, the Air Force, and the U.S. Army...all in one highly energized and extremely motivated package.

His staff, the Hearn Committee, was a direct extension of his enthusiasm and attention to detail and the next 18 months were to be the training of a lifetime for this young man from a privileged background who had so much to learn.

I will always be indebted to Billy Steele for his friendship, guidance, even his eccentricity. The thing that mattered most is the fact that Billy genuinely cared what happened to me and all his friends for that matter. You don't forget those people, although, upon my arrival at GMI, and my first encounter with George Hearn, I did have doubts!

OCS at Georgia Military Institute in the early 70's was another world entirely from anything I ever anticipated. The OCS staff seemed to have as their # 1 objective to make me and my fellow cadets *quit*, just get back in our vehicles and leave. Go home! Tuck tail and run! They yelled and screamed and made impossible demands and lot's of people stole away during the night to the safety and security of anyplace other than another minute with these "Hearn Committee Members...the Tactical Officers corps at GMI."

The temptation to give them their wish and just leave was ever present and very tempting!

Never having seen grown people act like these people did, I thought I would hang around and see what was coming next. I stayed and, in September 1971, I was commissioned as the youngest officer ever in the Georgia National Guard...a second lieutenant...by an act of Congress, no less.

One year later I was asked to come back and join the Hearn Committee. Asked to serve as a Tactical Officer myself for the next four years. Tells you something about my personality doesn't it!

Sometimes things work out, even though it might be quite some time before you are even aware of the fact.

You see, George Hearn has been my very dear and close friend throughout all these years. A crazier, brighter, more aggressive, and more giving person I have never known. He became a father, brother, harsh task-master and lifelong friend...just what the doctor ordered as the perfect prescription at that time in my life.

Eat Here & Get Gas!

Even as I write these words, George and I remain in touch with regular phone calls and visits...30 years and continuing.

George decided to retire in 1976 and I thought that would be a good military stopping point as well, so after seven years in the Guard, I became a full time civilian again with my military obligation honorably and satisfactorily completed.

My dad's untimely death and my close association with Billy Steele had come together in that automobile ride to the Atlanta airport to shape a future that I would not otherwise have known. The friendship, love, and support these very special people have provided me through all these years is immeasurable. The value of their counsel incalculable. The fact that it came about through that two hour trip to Atlanta is incredible.

I just wanted to be the Ford automobile dealer in Eastman. It didn't matter that it was 1976 and that Jimmy Carter was President. It didn't register with me that interest rates and the world economy were headed off into new and uncharted areas. De-regulation in the telephone and banking industry were not even possibilities at the time, but they both happened. Lines at gasoline stations were to be a common occurrence...and more. Much more!

Gerald Ford had just finished his very short term as President following Nixon's resignation and subsequent pardon. A fellow Georgian was in the White House. Things looked good to me!

I wanted things as they were planned for me years before. A University of Georgia graduate, an honorable military discharge. Let's sell cars and live happily ever after. Just that simple! I hadn't noticed my mother, Martha Skelton Williams, to be all that much like her mother. Somehow the "Skelton" factor is never too far from the surface. I didn't pay attention to the fact that my brother was drinking himself into a stupor several times each week and getting stoned on the off days from alcohol.

It didn't register with me that jobs were leaving our little community. Sell Fords! Make money! Make a great living! Live in a beautiful home at the edge of town! Vacation in Florida! Life and happiness and prosperity and family and everything as it should be…that's all I saw friend, **because that's all I looked for. That's all I wanted to see!**

It's funny how things can change, even imperceptibly…and all the more amazing how, given time and faith, things will eventually work out for the best.

With friends like Billy Steele, now a retired Brigadier General, and George Hearn, an active Juvenile Court Judge in Walton County…I knew things would be great. In fact, great and getting better all the time. All I could imagine was **GO GO**

Eat Here & Get Gas!

<u>**GO.**</u> This is America, the land of opportunity, right?. Work hard, keep the faith and things will work out right! Right? RIGHT?

I was just about to begin my term as a freshman pledge in HKU! In fact, classes had already begun and I was late to the first session.

A PhD from HKU

"You're late, you're late, for a very important date..."
George J. Hearn, III

Well, life is good again. It's the way things are supposed to be...just like the plan. No matter that our home place had been sold and our place at Daytona was sold and alcohol was appearing more and more frequently at my mother's house and my wife was pregnant and the notes at the bank on the Ford dealership were due and the floor-plan account with Ford Motor Credit was in arrears.

In my mind, life was back on the track I had seen in high school just a few short years before. All these problems were just opportunities that my personality and energy could resolve. Simple application problem. 'That Williams family tradition: Just go, go, go!

Somehow that concept didn't work very well when interest rates rose and the man who was my dad's partner in business and had himself run the business very successfully for 20 years, decided to sell his interest and go into direct competition with our family.

My education was underway and a degree from my dad's favorite university was forthcoming...he always said he was a graduate of the "School of hard knocks," or as he called it, HKU! I didn't know it then, but I had just been selected as a pledge in the freshman class.

In 1981, with interest rates at 21 percent the time came to decide either to go forward in the car business or cut our losses and close down; I chose the latter. Who knows if it was the right decision, but it was the decision I made based on the best information and judgment available at the time.

As I look back over the two decades since I made that decision, I think it was the right one, however, the fact is, it was a choice. There were several possibilities. All were considered in light of the times and circumstances, and I made the best decision I was capable of at the time under those conditions.

Was it right? Was it the best choice? Would things have turned out better had I made another choice? Different, certainly, but better? Who can say, and that's the point: Life is a series of choices, and, as you make them, each of us must move forward and live with the consequences of our decisions we either made or failed to make. Choosing wisely is a challenge and time will speak volumes of the quality of your choices.

Subsequent leases and increasing property values seem positive at this juncture, but who knows what the future holds?

Eat Here & Get Gas!

You see, long term learning is a part of HKU and you never seem to complete all the requirements for your degree. With more than three decades of opportunities in business, newspaper, banking and finance, and advertising under my belt, I believe I am quite a distance yet from graduation! However, it wasn't until I ignored the "You can't do that!; It ain't never been done before; and "You're gonna' fail" messages that a clear focus appeared on my horizon!

Deciding to start my own business was a turning point! This is America, friends. It's the land of opportunity. **GO-GO-GO!**

Charlotte and I were blessed with two sons, Chip, born in 1977 and Clint born in 1979, just at the end of my very challenging years in the Ford dealership.

Charlotte was working her way up the leadership trail in education in our county serving as curriculum director for the school system.

What a great time to build a house! Of course, two very small children, closing a family business, no particular income producing situation for me, and Charlotte really needed to complete the requirements for her specialist in education degree to be qualified for her next potential career assignment.

Yes! Of course! Let's commit to a large, long term high interest mortgage and really strap ourselves down...*right now!* And, like many young Americans then and now, that's just what we did.

Charlotte's dad's farm is a beautiful place and there was this one spot with the most perfect possibility for a 40-acre pond...and of course, that's the spot!

Jim Jamieson, Charlotte's uncle is a master of heavy equipment construction projects. For his niece, he built the most beautiful pond in the county. Thirty -seven acres of curves, trees, and an island at the north end. It was just beautiful. Never thought about keeping it mowed and pretty. It was just beautiful.

After it was completed, a concrete foundation for our home was laid, vast amounts of land clearing and yard building was undertaken. Spare no expense here, this was to be our **"Golden Pond"**, our vacation and retirement home! Where was the money to come from? Oh, something would come along. Remember, this is America, land of opportunity.

I shoveled dirt, planted grass, watered, vacuumed, cleaned house, kept two boys most days, and absolutely loved the time with Chip & Clint.

Charlotte went back to the University of Georgia and completed her degree requirements and was soon appointed to fill the office of superintendent of schools for the county.

Eat Here & Get Gas!

Interest rates began to settle back down just a bit, the grass began to cover our grounds, there was little or no furniture in our new home yet, and the monthly payments and expenses were teaching us great lessons on budgeting.

It was a great time, actually. Because I had time on my hands, I was most fortunate to develop a very close relationship with my boys, and I consider myself as particularly fortunate to have had that opportunity. It has lasted to this day.

My friend, Jim Williams, was a senior officer with a local bank and he had worked with me in the financial side of the automobile business.

When the decision to close that operation was reached, he created an opportunity for me to apply my public relations and advertising skills on a project for his bank.

It was a contract opportunity established for six months to meet specific objectives. By the end of the contract, Jim offered me a full-time position with his bank to handle similar public relations and advertising programs. **GO-GO-GO!**

One thing led to another, and my duties with the bank increased to include marketing, consumer lending, training, and public relations. It was a good situation and I might have continued with the bank for years but for the fact that the bank was closed on Wednesdays and that gave me an opportunity to either play golf or maybe sell something.

Charles M. Williams

Since my golf is limited, (I shoot in the low 80's 'cause if it gets any hotter than that I go where there is air conditioning), I spent my time creating newspaper and radio ad ideas. Then, on Wednesdays, I called on other banks in our area to sell those products! The ideas caught on and things began to look up for our little family and our businesses.

Macs! or Marketing Advertising Consulting Services was created in the late 1980s as the culmination of a long-held dream. Advertising was always at the core of my interest. Sales, marketing, talking…all a part of a bigger plan for me to follow. Creativity runs in our family and mine was just beginning to kick in…full-speed ahead, pedal to the metal…let's rock & roll! GO-GO-GO!

It is a successful business. Hundreds of companies have put their confidence in us to create and provide "Messages On Hold" and other advertising and public relations services for them…year after year.

Today, if you call banks, hospitals, car dealerships and many other businesses all across the country, you can hear me or some of our MACS associates voices when you are on hold, saying things like:

"Thank you for calling. The person you'd like to talk with will be with you in just a moment. Again,

Eat Here & Get Gas!

thanks for calling and thank you for patiently holding. We'll be right with you!"

It has been an excellent business product and has provided the opportunity for our company to expand into other areas of service.

Along with Messages On Hold, we produce national broadcast-quality, digital radio commercials. Using our creativity, about 100,000 digital sound effects, and a huge selection of licensed musical beds we have become pretty good at it!

It really is an impressive production capability and we have enjoyed tremendous success with these projects. We even have the capability of creating full campaign jingles with music and song. It's almost incredible when you think of all we offer…and where we are. Chauncey, Georgia just isn't on the tip of the tongue for most people looking for the kinds of services we offer. It ain't New York you know, but we do well!

If that isn't enough, we also create digital video productions for television commercials, corporate video productions, and training films. With today's technology in digital editing, we can actually create practically anything you can dream up, and have it appear, in motion, in color, just as you might imagine it, on video. And we can send that video image over the Internet.

Now, that is truly incredible.

Charles M. Williams

Want a newspaper layout for a bank campaign? Certainly! We can create it, produce it, have you approve it, print it to your publishing company which might be your local newspaper, print shop, or magazine publisher, anywhere in the country or around the world for that matter.

The amazing technology we have been able to harness is constantly improving. For example, sending a draft or a completed layout has become incredibly fast. Originally, we would write copy or produce an ad to meet a customer request. We would mail the layout to the customer, wait a few days and then call to get an opinion.

Then came the fax machine which certainly decreased the mail times and improved our service significantly. However, as new ideas and faster computers have become affordable and available, the Internet has become our primary delivery system.

Today, we create drafts and finished layouts, attach them to an e-mail message including color and even streaming audio and video files, and through electronic wizardry, have your ad appear exactly as you saw it, in your newspaper, on your radio station, on your telephone or wherever you direct us. The most amazing part is that this process can be accomplished literally in minutes…start to finish…where ever you or your business may be located.

Eat Here & Get Gas!

The most interesting fact about Macs is that the company could not have existed two decades ago. Yet today, it is a thriving business, literally out in the middle of nowhere...in the minds of most people.

And that, dear reader, is my point! Computers and the connections between them have literally made the world smaller and at the same time, the possibilities for still more new ideas is great and getting better every day!

It doesn't matter where you're located. What matters is your attitude, your willingness to try new ideas, new technologies, new ways of doing things. Genius is nothing more than seeing the same things everybody else sees...differently! There is very little under the sun that is actually new.

By that definition, MACS is indeed a "genius" company, but that's misleading. MACS is a wonderful group of people working in an incredible environment. For 15 years, our offices overlooked a beautiful 40-acre pond, 10 miles from town. (We were so far out in the country we mostly have to go toward town to hunt!)

Then we bought an abandoned Atlanta Gas Light building in our county seat town, Eastman. After an extensive remodeling project, we now have one of the most beautiful, spacious, and technologically advanced facilities for our operations that you could find anywhere.

Charles M. Williams

In fact, it is a surprise to most visitors to see what our capabilities are. And that has further enhanced our business. Virtual TV studios aren't on every corner in most small towns just yet you know. Blue Screen, Green Screen, sound stages, digital recording studios...not the everyday stuff you find in small, rural communities.

Our philosophy is simple: Customers always get more than they expect, period! Anything less is just not good enough.

The primary lesson I learned so far through HKU is deceptively simple. The difficult times forced me to stop; take a look around, and figure out what I was most interested in:

It was advertising of course.

I wanted to live in the community I grew up in.

I wanted to raise my sons to be self-sufficient "country-boys!"

I wanted to create advertising and marketing campaigns for businesses. Seems pretty simple when you see it written down like that, but that, friends is the starting point from which your future can be developed.

Can you imagine! People working together in this wonderful environment, creating high quality logos, advertisements, musical backgrounds, messages for telephone hold systems, corporate videos, live music...in a financially successful enterprise.

Folks, this is small town Georgia.

Eat Here & Get Gas!

Point is, it ain't **where** you are but ***what*** you are that counts.

In this marvelous day and age, you can be located practically anywhere…like we are.

Imagination is what it's all about. Use yours. Apply it! Try it!

See what you can do where you are right now.

You might be like us, pleasantly surprised. One thing is for sure: It doesn't' matter what part of the country you call home, the same principles apply!

Something about Fans

'You can pick your friends but God gave you your kinfolks.
Vernon Williams

My earliest days were spent just north of Eastman in a little frame house on the top of the hill a stone's throw from the city limit sign. That was in the early '50s and air conditioning was just finding its way into people's houses.

We had a big screened porch with an antique, (even then) ceiling fan that whirred and whirrled and made a sound like *err-err-err.*

I can remember standing under that old fan and looking up at it, copying the sound and spinning 'round and 'round with it.

I was just a little fellow (hard to believe I was ever a little fellow when you see me now), but I would stand there and spin 'round and 'round and 'round, and of course, I'd get dizzy and fall on the floor...waking up after a while on that cool porch with a breeze blowing over me. Oh, ya'll, I thought I was in heaven.

I guess that's where my love for screened porches with fans comes from. There is nothing to compare with such a place in my mind.

Even today, I like to stand under a fan and spin 'round and 'round and eventually fall, although if I do it much now, I break body parts.

It's about the same idea as drinking too much and falling on the floor with a couple of significant exceptions:

first, it doesn't cost as much.
Secondly, it isn't illegal.
Third, there is no hangover, unless of course, you bang your head against something on the way to the floor.
Best of all, you are just about as out of control as I ever was from drinking.
Alcohol and Charles don't mix!
I am, indeed, strange enough sober!
The difference between me and most other folks is that I recognize that fact!
Ten feet tall and bullet proof are feelings I can remember if only vaguely from my days with the bottle. I never drank to "get away" from anything but simply to drench myself with the mind numbing effects of "wobble water!"
That first belt of strong liquor was always harsh on the throat and burned all the way down to my deepest inside parts.
'Chase it with a little Coca Cola or Sprite (two great Georgia inventions), and the burning would stop shortly, or if it didn't, the second swig wouldn't require as much "chaser" anyway.
By the time the third swig came along, all in about 10 minutes, there was no noticeable burn to chase. Then it was just another swig and another

Eat Here & Get Gas!

and as you might guess, very shortly, the combined effect of the "swigs" was compounding.

I was in for a buzz that would quickly turn into a wobbly walk, slurred speech, and the self concept of absolutely "Ten feet Tall and Bullet Proof" Just about as far from what I actually would be as day is from night, but I didn't know that! I notice most drunks don't know that either.

There are lots of funny stories about people who drink too much. Unfortunately, the truth is, it's a bad choice. Not one person out of all the billions who have tried liquor over the centuries, not one has ever beaten it–and a much more significant observation is this: it won't be you!

The facts are just too clear: if you get into alcohol, it will win, sooner or later. Count on it. There is a life lesson there somewhere. Think of the people you know who started out drinking socially or to gain acceptance to one group or another. Was that a good choice? Did it eventually turn out to be a good choice?

Is any group or social occasion really worth the very real possibilities and potential consequences of intoxication, driving under the influence, or maybe even involuntary manslaughter?

Someone's life could be at risk for your decision. Someone's life could be lost. That someone could be you, or someone close to you or someone close to somebody! I don't mean to be short but from my perspective, the facts and statistics are painfully clear. "**Alcohol ruins people's lives. It is a <u>bad choice</u>**".

With that thought in mind, let me tell you about a personal experience with alcohol. I have spent a few nights with my arm around the bowl of a cool porcelain commode just hoping my toenails would come through and scrape everything from my insides out and into the cool, clean, waiting receiver in the hope that such an action might bring some relief. Those are really pleasant memories. Whew! I hope you can't identify with them and if not, don't go there.

Where did I get the idea that alcohol was a good choice? As a child I watched my parents. To them, a few drinks with friends before dinner, a few with dinner and a few more after dinner was as natural as forks, napkins and Lucy Ricardo's California dinnerware!

It's just what they did. It was a part of the "successful" lifestyle. Everybody did it. In fact, the only ones who didn't imbibe were those "squeaky clean" people, you know, the ones nobody really likes to be around. Those who were not a part of the "in crowd."

I saw what alcohol did to people first hand. I watched my folks use it at virtually every opportunity. I was amazed there were no serious automobile accidents, broken bones, or fires. Everything was in place on many occasions. God just wasn't ready for them at that time.

Eat Here & Get Gas!

My in-laws were in stark contrast to my own parents. Alcohol was not and never had been present in their home. Mr. Cadwell didn't and still doesn't even drink iced tea, truly a Southern delicacy when it is sweetened just right!

I have long recognized my good fortune to stand at the point of decision as the great poet Robert Frost described: "Two roads diverged in a yellow wood, and I, I took the one less traveled by, and that has made all the difference."

I know the pathway he was describing and consider myself highly fortunate to have "come this way!"

If you haven't come to the conclusion just yet that alcohol and the various other drugs that are available are a bad choice, don't beat yourself up over it. Just think it through. Give yourself a little time. Let go any pain or regret you still carry over the fact that you are currently addicted and begin the process of moving forward. There is hope. There is help. There is a future without the pain.

All these addictions are in some ways like that old ceiling fan I mentioned earlier. They can make you feel good for a while, even put you in a dream or mesmerized state, for a while. They can and will spin you 'round and 'round and 'round until you find yourself falling.

The difference is, the effect of the fan will disappear in a few moments. With addictions, this is just the beginning…and the fall can be forever.

Black Iron Skillet

The greatest of these is love
I Corinthians, Chapter 13

Sometimes, the best gifts are the simplest ones! In the small town rural south *(and I suppose it's true around the rest of the country)* when young couples announce their wedding plans, bridal registries are established.

These registries are a wedding tradition. Local gift shops and stores that sell dishes and jewelry and things people buy to give as wedding gifts set up special tables for friends and family to come by and see what the bride and groom (not) have selected.

The idea is to have friends and family "add to the pattern" with their gift selections, Nice plan! Pretty paper! Beautiful "stuff" that most guys could not name if their lives depended on it. But it happens. It is tradition! It is probably universal, and I think it is great! I would bet the original idea came from the south! I don't know, but it seems like a good bet to me!

When Charlotte and I were planning to get married, sure enough, there were bridal registries set up. Friends and family gave us gifts of the china "we" selected, according to plan! Great "stuff"! We still have it in a cabinet and take it out to wash (occasionally). 'Very few times we've ever used it, but it is there and it is beautiful.

As our wedding day approached, there were lots of presents. There was one table just about full of those pretty white boxes with fancy paper and shiny ribbons and one most unusual sight: a used, black-iron skillet.

I wasn't exactly sure why someone would give us a used frying pan as a gift and it did look out of place among all those pretty new packages.

Of course, we had no idea that a "new" frying pan was a real chore to break in right, and that it could take lots of work and effort to get one to the point that "sticking" was virtually eliminated. This was, of course, before technological advances such as "teflon" and "Pam"!

I wondered about that gift and made it a point to find out where it came from! There was no card attached and no one seemed to know who had brought the old skillet. In the rush of activity surrounding the wedding, the mystery didn't keep a spot on the "front burner" of my mind. There were a few other things along about that time!

It's been more than 30 years since those heady pre-wedding days, and most of the gifts have been appreciated but stored for most of that time. In fact, some of them were only seen when we were busy packing up to move to a new home.

However, that old black-iron skillet has never spent more than a few hours in a cabinet. The

Eat Here & Get Gas!

hamburgers and sausage that thing has cooked over the years is only rivaled by the pancakes and thin corn-bread slices it has delivered.

One look at my waistline and you can see that old skillet has been hard at work! It is a family treasure and will likely be around as long as we are, and then some!

Where it came from remained a bit of a mystery. It just appeared at the right time and seemed somehow out of place and yet, it has endured for our entire married lives! What a unique gift! A used, black-iron skillet!

The person who gave this most unusual item is herself, unique. Giving is what her entire life has been about and in fact, it still is! She is one of the most beautiful people I have ever had the pleasure to know, and I have known her all my life.

'Turns out, this lady lives in a little cottage just at the north edge of Eastman. The city limit line runs almost right through her front porch. She and her husband lived in this house since back in the early '40s, and maybe even longer. 'Very likely, she has lived in this same house all her adult life.

The house I grew up in is only a half mile further out from town, so I can remember this lady from my very earliest years, but not just from passing by on the way to town and back. Indeed not! She always stopped by our house, and I never saw her without some beautiful tomatoes or squash or some other very special gift for my parents.

Her husband was an automobile mechanic and a very good one at that. Unfortunately, he worked on General Motors vehicles and being the son of the local Ford dealer, that was brand "X" at our house!

Oh, Mr. Fred could fix anything and was one of the most dependable people I ever knew! Today, he would not be called a "mechanic" but a "service technician". The big difference is that back then, "mechanics" could actually figure out what was wrong with your car and fix it.

This couple never had children of their own. They lived together in their cottage and went about doing things for other people, like her mother, his folks, and the list just grew and grew. She worked in a popular men's store in town for years and years until that store closed. Everybody I knew just loved to go in there. She always made everyone feel so special.

To say that she was a great salesperson doesn't begin to describe her! Patrons left that store with a brand new self image and everyone knew a very special someone who really cared for you had met your need for clothes—*and a whole lot more!*

Did she throw up her hands and quit when that store went out of business? Of course not! She went to work as a clerk in a local meat market and guess what–before long, there were people lined

Eat Here & Get Gas!

up to have her wait on them with choice sausages, steaks, and so much more.

There was something very special about this lady and everyone who had the privilege of coming in contact with her knew it!

Years passed and eventually the meat store's owner's health resulted in the closing of the business. In fact, about that same time in 1978, this dear woman's husband passed away. For most people, that would have been the time to throw in the towel and just quit working, and maybe just give up on life itself. After all, age was a factor. Some disabilities were present.

But did she quit? Of course not! She just went to work again, this time taking her loving personality and that ever-present, wonderful smile to people much less fortunate than she. In fact, for the past 20 years or so, she spent almost every night "sitting" with people in the community who need her assistance.

Nursing homes, private homes, wherever she is needed, that's where you'll find her, always looking for a little something she can do to make someone's life just a little better. Most of the time, just knowing how much she cares is enough. She does everything from that self-less perspective.

You see, all those years ago, this lady knew how to prepare a frying pan for years and years of dependable service. She also knew that young couples would not know how to do that job, or even that it needed to be done! So she gave us her very own black-iron skillet. It was not a beautiful, new, or expensive gift. Instead, she gave us the most beautiful gift of all, her personal gift of love.

Even though this couple never had children of their own, she always treated me like her own, just as she did my sister, my brother, and no telling how many other people in our community and beyond.

She was never rich by today's standards. She has never been defeated by set backs. Ever! She doesn't give up! No, sir! She has always applied herself to helping others, the same thing she's done every day of her life!

She doesn't have a big family. She has little interest in politics. She doesn't have a big home or a fancy car, and she has never missed calling me on my birthday, in more than fifty-two years—and counting!

In fact, there is no telling just how many people she remembers with birthday greetings in her own very special and loving way every day of the year! Just a phone call that always starts with, "Hey, Honey!"

She may not be rich with "things" and "stuff." but oh, she has great wealth!

She has people all around this area, and who knows where else, whose lives she has touched with her thoughtfulness. What she gives can't be sold for money or traded for things of value, but they are among the most prized possessions of a lifetime. To be one of her adopted children puts you in a huge family of people who adore her.

My favorite example of her very special gifts is this old, used, black-iron skillet "Miss Irene" gave to Charlotte and me as a wedding gift so many years ago.

Of course, I am talking about "Miss Irene Chance," (Mrs. Fred Chance) of Eastman. That old frying pan will be around all my years to remind me of "Miss Irene" and her totally unpretentious, unselfish, and loving ways.

'Fact is, I'm looking forward to hearing from her when my birthday comes around again, and I can just bet there are lots and lots of people who feel the same!

Happy Birthday, Miss Irene! (May 31st). I am so glad to be on your list. I used my old skillet this morning! I love you!

It ain't wrong...Its jus' different!

There is something very special about the South
Mark Twain

It's a fact that most people in the South unconsciously break sentences with an occasional bottom lip opened to one side or the other of our noses!

You see, in this part of the country, a blast of air in front of first, one eye, and then the other (the order is dictated by the congestion and traffic) is a fundamental necessity in the summer, particularly during the dog days August and September.

Granted, people unfamiliar with this phenomenon are somewhat confused when they first observe it, but given time, they not only understand, they actually embrace and wholeheartedly adopt the practice.

As a private pilot, a friend asked me to fly to Macon and pick up the wife of one of his employees and bring her to Eastman.

I was just starting out as a pilot. I thought it would be a great chance for me to get a little flight time on someone else's nickel. I flew the little Cessna into Macon, found my passenger, got her bags, and made ready to fly back to Eastman, about a 25-minute airplane ride in a Cessna 172.

The lady was from the north and this was her first trip to Georgia. She didn't talk like us. In fact, when she said the word talk, she actually said: "TAW-AK!" Now I think that's funny.

I kinda' like to listen to people who aren't from here! It ain't wrong, it's just different as Willie Nelson said in the country song, "Momma, don't let your babies grow up to be cowboys!"

All the preparations were made, we were taxied into position, and the tower cleared us for take-off. Just as we rolled down the runway and picked up speed, she asked the question in her other-than-Southern accent, "Mr. Williams, what would you consider the most unusual thing I will notice about people in this part of the country?"

I could feel the little Cessna beginning to lift just slightly as the airspeed increased over the wings, I responded, "Well, *(Pfffffffffftttttttttttt)* I think *(Pfffffffffftttttttttttt)* you'll notice most people *(Pfffffffffftttttttttttt)* especially this time of year *(Pfffffffffftttttttttttt)* seem to talk with *(Pfffffffffftttttttttttt)* what you might consider Pfffffffffftttttttttttt) an annoying (Pfffffffffftttttttttttt) little habit.

(Pfffffffffftttttttttttt)

At that precise moment, the little Cessna sprung up off the runway and we were climbing at it's maximum capability.

Eat Here & Get Gas!

I happened to notice this lady's color change to a pale, putty tone. Her knuckles were white with her fists clenched and she froze into a very stiff position. I could just imagine the thoughts in her mind: "My God, what kind of fool have I crawled into an airplane with?" (I expected that sort of thinking, as that's what I was always used to with my wife and my mother whenever they flew with me, so I figured that's about what she was thinking!)

'Fact is, she never said a word the entire flight. She remained frozen with her eyes glazed over and looked straight ahead, never even looking when I flew over particular landmarks and told her about them.

When we landed, she was visibly relieved to be back on the ground. She quickly moved away from me and the little airplane.

It was about a month later in fact in late September before I happened to see her again. She said, "Mr. Williams *(Pfffffffffftttttttttttt)* it took me a while *(Pfffffffffftttttttttttt)* but I now understand *(Pfffffffffftttttttttttt)* exactly what you were talking about *(Pfffffffffftttttttttttt)* in the airplane that day *(Pfffffffffftttttttttttt)* and you know, *(Pfffffffffftttttttttttt)* I think you were right *(Pfffffffffftttttttttttt)*." She had encountered one of the South's worst phenomena, gnats, and learned to deal with them.

It's called adapting! It is necessary and it does work in any situation. This lady adapted to her new surroundings. It wasn't easy. There was a process of change involved. She was even shocked at first, but she adapted and we became and remain good friends, though I think she still likes a little more than the normal amount of space between us!

Over the years, I have learned that each of us has to adapt to changing circumstances, at least until we can know enough about them to either change the situation, eliminate it, or move away from it. Gnats are just one of those things. I understand they don't exist above the Gnat-Line, which runs east to west just about through the middle of Macon (the gnats live south of Macon). I have always wanted some politician to commit to redrawing the Gnat-Line as a part of his or her political platform, but so far, no one has been willing. Of course, there is always hope for the next generation of politicians and gnat haters! I might catch one in a week moment and get such a promise out of him or her!

Whether or not the Gnat Line ever changed, I am willing to bet there is some equally-annoying creature or thing that lives in just about every part of the world, every where, every day.

When you think about it, Gnats ain't so *(Pfffffffffftttttttttttt)* bad after all. At least they don't bite!

Eat Here & Get Gas!

Of course, we have mosquitoes and "Can't see-'ems" for that! But, I ain't moving!

I believe in the concept: It ain't where you are outside but what you are inside that counts and that goes a long way toward determining where and who you are in life—*(Pffffffffftttttttttttt)*.

By the way, according to my good friend and successfully published author Ed Grisamore, a sure way to get rid of gnats swarming in your face is to cut a hole in the seat of your pants.

Point to ponder ain't it!

Millionaire's Island

"I don't want to be a millionaire, I just want to live like one!"
Vernon Williams

Sara and Cooper had a daughter named "Little Sara" and a younger daughter *(regretfully a few years older than me)* named Mary Ann.

From the time I was about six or seven, (1957-58) our families went to Jekyll Island each year to spend a few days together.

Jekyll Island was unique. It was a privately-owned island for decades, but during World War II and the sighting of German U-boats off the coast of Jekyll, it was decided that the really rich people shouldn't go there any more.

The island was basically abandoned and in the early 1950s it was donated to the State of Georgia. Of course the state took it, built a causeway over to it (up until then the only access had been by boat) and now the bourgeoning middle class began driving over to it in automobiles.

Lucy and Ricky, the TV Ricardos, were driving across America, pulling a house trailer. But folks in South Georgia drove their vehicles (all shapes and descriptions) to the coast to spend a few days on the beach with the world's absolute largest horseflies! There was little else on Jekyll in the late 1950s. The millionaire's village was largely in ruins. One motel, the "Wanderer," was available for vacations and there was this beach, we named it Horsefly Cove!

Even so, it was great! Little Sara, Mary Ann, my brother, Verne, and my sister, Pat, always rode together in dad's convertible with the top down and listened to the "BIG APE," WAPE Radio out of Jacksonville, Florida.

It was so exciting to get south of McRae and be able to pick up the scratchy signal from WAPE and hear the "APE call" they used as a signature.

WaaaaaaaaaaaaaaaaaEEEEEEEEEEEEaaaa aaaaahhhhhhhhhhhh!

It was powerful! It kinda' made me think of "Big Sara's" laugh. The Big APE played rock and roll for the beach-going teenagers and we would almost dance in the car as we rode down the two-lane all the way to Jekyll.

The Island had been nicknamed "Millionaire's Island" because for decades, the only people with access were the super-rich. America's wealthiest families from the 19th century, the Rockerfellers, the Goodyears, JP Morgan, and others.

Jekyll had been discovered and developed as a rich man's paradise. Cottages were actually expansive, beautiful, ultra-modern homes with every convenience, including elevators and other innovations. The "millionaires club" was organized to operate the island and one of America's first condominium complexes was designed and built

Eat Here & Get Gas!

to accommodate those members who wanted the privileges of club membership and cottage ownership but, for whatever reason, elected not to build a mansion comparable to the really rich folks, the Rockerfellers, the Goodyears, etc.

Today, the old condominium complex is something to see. The Radison Corporation purchased the run-down property and transformed it into one of the most attractive and historic vacation locations on the east coast. The facility faces west toward the Jekyll River and is set among the beautiful live oaks interspersed with Georgia pines.

Spanish moss is everywhere. It is a charming and pleasant place. Opulence was the word. Money was no object. Imagination was in large supply and the island was the place to be for wonderful climate, abundant hunting and fishing, and seclusion. Remember, you couldn't get there without a boat. And not just any boat would do. Big boats were very much the rage and these people had the money to compete, *lavishly!*

The cottages today are fully restored and maintained as tourist attractions by the state of Georgia and are easily worth the trip to Jekyll. People come just to get to see one of America's best kept secrets and to see how the "millionaires" of the last century enjoyed their leisure time.

Just a note: J.P. Morgan had a fully enclosed tennis court constructed just behind his "cottage" and the facility is in perfect repair and still in use today. In fact, you can schedule time for a match if you're visiting "millionaire's village!"

As kids, we weren't concerned with all that! History was what you had to read in school and we thought we were the millionaire's children anyway!

It was fun to swim in the old Millionaire Village pool and sneak through the dilapidated condominium complex, but much more important and interesting to us was the art of building sand-castles.

We fried our skin on the beach and went back to our room at the Wanderer to enjoy *air-conditioning* and freeze our rears off.

Sara and Cooper and Martha and Vernon hung around the room and enjoyed the cool air. Quite naturally, there were several well-hidden bottles of Ancient Age, Jack Daniels, Smirnoff's and Evan Williams. I figured my dad felt a special closeness with ole' Evan. It stayed with him most of his short life. Probably the combination of fried foods, no exercise, lots of partying, and heavy smoking contributed, and together, the combination was thorough. I didn't know I was observing these bad habits, but of course, I was. Although for a time I jumped into that lifestyle with both feet, fortunately, I saw a different lifestyle away from alcohol and other drugs, and have followed that path successfully for decades.

Eat Here & Get Gas!

Jekyll will always hold a very special place for me, all those trips; Little Sara with her delightfully-Southern tones and the absolutely gorgeous Southern belle, Mary Ann. She was my earliest recollection of absolute perfection.

A young boy's dreams and fantasies are beyond wonderful and well beyond my limited vocabulary. (At least that's a good excuse for me not to get in too deep here. Not sure my wife would understand you know!) Even though they are now memories, they are still quite clear.

From miniature golf and little gasoline engine "Peco" automobiles…I begged and begged to get one of those to take home to no avail.

Tommy Nicholson had one. He lived across from my grandmother Williams and I looked forward to visiting my grandmother since I knew I might get a ride in Tommy's great "Peco"! 'Didn't happen much, but when it did, it was fabulous! I remember the excitement 45 years later!

Jekyll will always hold a special place in my memories. Years later Charlotte and I got engaged on the island and spent lots of summer nights walking that wonderful beach (they got rid of the huge horseflies).

Today, Jekyll is perfectly beautiful. The island is only nine miles long and just over a half mile wide. The bicycle trail around the entire island is only 18 miles long and my family has ridden it many times.

It was and is a place of peace and tranquility, a place you could feel comfortable allowing your kids to run and explore without so much concern for their safety.

Thinking back on it now, Jekyll Island is a great memory. It was just one part of our family's enduring friendship with Sara and Cooper Norris and their beautiful daughters—have you figured out that I had a kid's crush on Mary Anne. *Oh yes, me and every other boy in Eastman!*

NOTE: Mary Ann married a fine guy, a pharmacist and lives in Alabama. She has raised a family and led quite a successful life. In fact, I saw her this past year and can tell you, she hasn't lost a step in any department! Dream girls seldom do you know!

As I think of those times years ago with the Norris family, my favorite memory of Sara and Cooper still makes me laugh! It seems they always came to eat supper with my folks on Christmas Eve. It was always a festive occasion and a time to thoroughly enjoy the spirit (and spirits) of the holidays at our house.

Of course, as every little kid was well aware, I knew everyone had to be quiet, in bed, and asleep before Santa would come. I also knew Santa was watching and listening closely to make sure everyone *was* asleep!

The training had been thorough and effective. I knew these facts were real and that the little fat man would not come if all were not quiet and sound asleep.

Confident of having met my obligations of a clean room, good bath, and eating all my supper, I dashed to my bed after giving all the people around the table a big hug.

"That's a good hug, BIG MAN" as Cooper always yelled! He was a car salesman who worked with my dad in the automobile business. He was a loveable older guy and always had a big smile and an especially wonderful laugh. Very distinctive. His whole body was taken over by his laughter.

His wife Sara was a well educated person. She was a teacher. I always dreaded being around her in school because I knew she and my mother were close and anything I did would go straight back home to roost.

Sara was a wonderful cook. My mother, who never went to college, although she always told people she "went to Wesleyan" in Macon, (actually she went with my sister when she was a student there, and to TIFT College in Forsyth, and to Middle Georgia College in Cochran, (my brother was the student) and to Georgia Southern in Statesboro, (yep, that was my brother, too,) and to the University of Georgia in Athens, (that was my brother, my wife and me). You get the idea. My mother always admired Sara for her education and meticulous and wonderful cooking and kitchen habits.

Sara made the best biscuits in the world and it seems to me she always made them on Christmas Eve.

Big Sara was a large woman with Lucy Ricardo hair and the diaphragm power of a medium-bull-elephant. When she would get tickled, and she could do that in a heartbeat, she could laugh loudly enough for the people in the next county to hear and be startled. It wasn't any ordinary laugh. It was more like a two-cycle engine being revved up without a muffler, just a *wwwwaaaaaaahhhhhhHHHHHHHHHHHHHHHHH* sound that would, I thought, easily wake the dead, and especially little children trying to go to sleep so Santa Claus could come…like guess who?

I just knew Santa could actually hear her laugh at the North Pole!

Christmas Eve was a great time for guests at supper. Northerners, well educated, white-collar folks call it dinner but Southern folks like us called the meal at twelve noon.

Somehow we all got breakfast down as breakfast all over the country but those other two have been a source of confusion for generations.

Well, back to Christmas. Just as I would begin to doze off, Sara would deliver a "two-cycle chain-saw-at-full-throttle-with-no-muffler" laugh from the front of the house.

Eat Here & Get Gas!

You would have to see that house to truly appreciate her power. That house was more than 200 feet from the dining area to my bedroom, but the walls themselves would reverberate.

I just knew Santa would hear that laugh from the North Pole and say, "Oh to heck with it for that house this year," but somehow, I would fall into a deep sleep and wake up to find, once again, that he had been there last night and didn't forget to bring me a thing I had asked for. *And clothes.*

I guess the loud noise did create some confusion for the old elf, I never asked for clothes!

I know now that our families were not real millionaires. My dad's favorite saying was that "I don't want to be a millionaire…I just want to live like one!"

Friends, you can believe he did just that and more. He spent his life making sure our family felt special. He treated us all as if we were the finest people on earth. He did that with all his friends and relatives and he made everyone he came in contact feel that they were the most important people on earth in his eyes.

'Fact is, we didn't really need to be millionaires in terms of financial assets. We had so much more. Every one of us knew we were loved. We had everything and then some that we needed. Even better, we had air-conditioning in our homes and cars. J.P. Morgan had a nice "cottage" and one heck of a boat, he might have even owned

Charles M. Williams

Jekyll Island—but he never had air-conditioning! Probably never met anyone better looking than Mary Ann, and I can guarantee you he never heard either the Big Ape call or Big Sara's incredible and unforgettable laugh. Poor guy!

Ahab & Clyde

You know, it just don't get much more inspirin' than that!
CMW

Over the past few years I have had the tremendous privilege of speaking, telling jokes, picking a guitar, and singing for groups all across the southeast and around the country. What an incredible experience that is and what a challenge. I love it more than anything else I get to do...and that is saying something! I have absolutely absorbed the antics of my favorite entertainers. All of them!

I started out listening to Brother Dave Gardner, "Rejoice Dear Hearts," and his delightful tales about the "Origins of Rock-And-Roll". You remember! When "Little David went off to carry kosher food to his brothers *what wuz* engaged in battle with the Piladelphians and how them Philadelphians had done "run in a *GIANT* on 'em named *Goliath!*" What a story!

Ray Stevens' first record, *"Ahab the Arab"* caught my fancy and I instantly memorized that sack full of words. Ray is a fellow Georgian and the fact that he, like Dave Gardner, was easily able to change himself into several characters, right before your "ears" and "eyes" just captured my imagination. It facinated me. I wanted to do that so badly! I practiced and practiced and practiced. All the time, anywhere, for anybody that would humor me by not walking off or throwing things, at least not messy things.

In fact, the first time I can remember "performing" was for my parents and of course, I did *"Ahab!"* Pretty soon I was doing that song in my school classes and for the "assemblies." You better bet I was hooked for life!

As a guitarist, Chet Atkins set the standard. He was the master and I doubt whether he will ever be approached...let alone surpassed! Duayne Eddie was out there. The Beach Boys, and of course, my dear brother Verne, for real, were all guitar icons for me.

As a story teller, Dr. Carl Hurley holds my attention more than anyone else for a deceptively simple reason: he gets just as tickled and enjoys his materials every bit as much as his audiences. Jeff Foxworthy, yet another Georgia entertainer, is delightful. He has taken the concept of "Redneck'ism" to heights never before considered.

Listen, when I am fortunate enough to hear somebody tell a good story or pick a song I think I can do, I try my best. I look for stories and ideas and methods everywhere! When I find 'em, I do my best to learn 'em and deliver 'em to my next audience through my own methods of course!

Audiences vary. Most groups seem to readily identify with the material I am most comfortable

Eat Here & Get Gas!

with. Diverse groups seem to take some offense to some of the comments I make about odd behavior among certain groups. I need to work on that I know. Really good guitar pickers have been kind in not telling me how badly I need to improve if I plan to continue calling myself a guitar picker. People who have great singing voices and know music and all that have been equally kind and patient with me. Good story-tellers have yet to chastize me.

You know there is something I am ever so slowly learning! I have come to the sad but true conclusion that I will never pick a guitar as well as Chet Atkins. For that matter, I doubt anyone else will either! Fact is, I realize I don't have to! I only have to pick as well as I am capable of picking. I have come to the realization that I can't expect to sing as well as Ray Stevens or George Strait, or Randy Travis, or any other known, recognized singer. The wonderful fact is again, I don't have to.

What I DO have to do is sing to the best of *Charles Williams'* abilities! Now, when I get up to tell stories, I know I don't do it as well as Brother Dave or Jeff Foxworthy or Dr. Carl Hurley. But you know the answer! Right! And if I could just pass that wonderful realization along to every group, every individual that I come in contact with, what a revelation and a revolution in personal freedom would follow.

Charles M. Williams

I think we all squat and strain and push ourselves to absolutely impossible standards. How many Vince Gills can there be???? ONE, and it ain't me! How many Chet Atkins can there be? One, and again, that ain't me! But, How many Charles Williams can there be? Same answer of course, ONE. But, that I can do and the revelation is, I can do that better than anybody! If I give my best as a singer, picker, story teller and individual to my audiences. It always is, as Art Williams, the insurance giant says, enough! I believe audiences would rather see a first rate ME than me doing a third rate imitation of somebody I ain't never gonna be. So far so good!

Sadly, I don't think most people ever come to that realization and spend enormous amounts of energy, both mental and physical, all sorts of consternation, suffer failure after failure and defeat after defeat battling an immovable object. As the brilliant Alka-Seltzer ad writers said in the sixties: "OH WHAT A RELIEF IT IS!" I only hope you can imagine. I still strive to please my audiences. Even more than ever before and I will always have that certain amount of fear as I step up to perform for a group. But now, I look forward to being me and offering them the very best I have at that time! You just can't believe the difference. You cannot believe the relief. There will always be tension...I think if you don't have tension something must not be functioning just right...but now, I just can't wait!

Eat Here & Get Gas!

I want to share ideas and excitement about the things I have learned! Music, stories, lessons, finger-style picking. What a difference a little self acceptance can make. What I would give to be able to help you grasp the power of this idea in whatever it is you do! Wow!

If you want to learn to get up and talk or tell jokes, or play music, or sing, or emcee, or teach, you first just have to get up and do it. So what if it doesn't work perfectly the first time? So what if you make mistakes? So what if you fall flat on your face? If it's what you really want to do, just pick yourself up, brush yourself off and go at it again!

I figured out as a kid that the worst that could happen never happens! Anything less is better than the worst that could happen. So, what are you waiting for?? Give it a try. See what happens. You just might enjoy yourself!

Little Jack

Friends are friends forever...
Michael W. Smith

One of my earliest best friends was Little Jack Eckles. Nothing about him was little, especially his smile and his mischief. He was called "Little Jack" because his daddy was a big man and, as is the Southern way, was referred to as "Big Jack". He was a particularly large fellow, especially to a little kid of eight or 10, such as Little Jack and I were when we spent days together at each other's houses to play.

Little Jack's house amazed me. Big Jack was involved in law enforcement. He worked with the local sheriff's department and had the most interesting things around the house. All kinds of firearms, firecrackers, knives, brass knuckles, and real hand cuffs. There was even an old hearse, an early '50s Cadillac ambulance kept for its value as a shrine parade and family vacation mobile. It was the original "sport utility vehicle"!

My imagination soared whenever I was with Little Jack. He always had something unique to show, do, or talk about. Going to his house was a particular treat because I never knew what to expect. Most of my friends called *my* house the "Smithsonian" because my mother was something beyond an immaculate house keeper. I was often required to strip off at the garage, leave my "filthy" clothes in the laundry room and run naked through the house to the other end for a bath. Of course Sara and Cooper or Marsden and Nanny or Bud and Eola or Albert and Edith, or any or all of these friends of my folks might be enjoying a toddie.

Here I would come, streaking through, even though I hadn't heard of that act at the time!

The "Smithsonian" was a beautiful place and was an experience within itself to grow up in. There's probably a lot to do with my psyche in there somewhere.

Jack's house was all the more exhilarating and particlularly liberating to me. One day, "Miss Ione", Jack's mother, fixed a dinner for us (noon meal, remember, this is the south–stay *wimmie* now) and everybody, including Big Jack, was seated around the big brown kitchen table.

As is the Southern custom, a blessing was offered and the bowls of wonderful Southern cooking were passed around the table. (No doubt a contributing factor to my life-long battle with weight. I have lost hundreds of pounds. Trouble is, I have also gained hundreds, plus a few more and that keeps me above what I would like to be!)

Little Jack and I were at one end of the table and Big Jack was at the other end. As the meal progressed with delicious "sweet tea" as you can find only in the heart of the south, I wanted another

Eat Here & Get Gas!

one of "Miss Ione's" (*That's pronounced "eye-own" with equal accents, slightly more on the first syllable*) hot, buttery rolls.

Friends, my Smithsonian training took over and I said loudly enough for everyone to hear, "Would you pass the rolls, please?" Very polite! Just right! Martha would have been so proud! Her training had taken hold and her youngest had done well. I was almost beaming my own self!

'Turns out Big Jack had not been through the rigorous "Smithsonian Prep School" and responded to my request with a hard, fast-ball pitch of one of Miss Ione's biggest and best biscuits which seemed to whistle as it flew from his end of the table squarely at my face.

Of course, Miss Ione reprimanded Big Jack as only a sweet Southern lady could do, and of course, it was to no avail because he thought it was almost as funny as Little Jack and I did.

The fact that such an incident would have brought immediate and total banishment from the Smithsonian made it all the more hilarious to me at the time, and I have remembered it since as another happy memory of childhood, mine and Big Jack's.

More than anything, that event made me realize early on that the big grown people are really just kids who have more to do than just cut-up, play, and have a good time. I've tried to keep that idea in mind ever since! So far so good!

Charles M. Williams

All of us love and are attracted to things that are different. For that and other reasons, Little Jack loved to come to the "Smithsonian".

We even talked about ordering some of those 4 inch diameter felt ropes with the brass hooks on the ends and draping them across doorways in my mother's grand house to help guide the tours of people from Good Housekeeping and Southern Living as they would constantly come through and "ooohed and ahhhed" at this beautiful home. *(They never really came, but in my mother's mind, we had to be prepared at all times!)*

It really was and still is a very pretty place, even if the plans were upside down when Oscar Harris poured the concrete. The beautiful front door part faces the railroad out back. The back area with the huge living room faces the highway across the pond. Even so, it couldn't be a more beautiful place and it remains a landmark in this part of the country. Jim Spradley came to Eastman in the early 70's when Pet Milk had bought Stuckeys. He bought the house and lives there today!

However, in the eyes of a kid and all his little mischievous friends, it was quite out of the ordinary. Unusual. Different. Jack and most of my other friends especially loved that difference.

My mother was a fastidious housekeeper, to say the least. Every single day, without exception, she could be found operating a huge Electrolux

Eat Here & Get Gas!

machine and vacuumed under, over, around, and through every part of the house.

That old machine was the only alarm clock I ever heard and believe me, it easily woke-up people in the house on the hill above us and everybody between, except, of course, my older brother.

Martha got that vacuum going as she made beds, cooked breakfast, cleaned windows, and washed her new "T" Bird.

Trust me, all that work was just a preparation, a warm up exercise if you will, to getting into her precious yards to plant, replant, weed, seed, and breed plants with names nobody knew.

Her daily routine was absolutely a schedule. It was endless. It was like clockwork. She was well beyond busy. And of course, these jobs had to be completed in time for her to prepare breakfast, lunch, dinner, snacks, and be a car-pool operator, a taxi-service for three children, and the ultimate hostess each afternoon when Sara and Cooper or Marsden and Nanny, or Albert and Edith, or Bud and Eola, or all or some combination of this group convened for the day's cocktails at the Smithsonian or wherever else.

Needless to say, my mother's highly developed organizational skills were well ingrained in me. My days in the military were a snap. You can bet I could make a bed, take out trash, police an area, and on and on! I excelled in my early military training. It was just like home! I wondered why anyone complained. I thought it was business as usual!

However, the high degree of organization she followed created a clearly discernable pattern that even as kids, Little Jack and I recognized. And found ways to take advantage of our intelligence information.

Little Jack came over to the Smithsonian one Friday. Miss Ione dropped him off to spend the afternoon with me. On this particular day, he didn't just have his usual few few firecrackers, which was a common occurrence with Little Jack. This time, he had something unique. He had a firecracker with a string that came out of both ends. Essentially, you could snatch the two strings away from each other and that would cause a rather loud explosion.

This was in the early 1960s, remember! Times were good. We were two little boys getting into mischief! Of course it was a foretaste of things to come, but for now, it was just pure fun!

My mother's Friday schedule was well-documented and we had previously and very carefully observed her routine. The little string-poppers were just the thing to conjure up thoughts of mischief in our little minds.

The garage to the Smithsonian was at the north end of the house and it had a little ramp to bring a

Eat Here & Get Gas!

vehicle up to the floor level from the driveway. The end of the garage was a solid brick wall.

My mother's parking place was the "right-hand-side" of this two-car masterpiece and my dad's space was on the left. In the center of the garage was a screen door that opened away from my mother's side and led to another door that opened to the laundry room. Very neat arrangement. *(The laundry room was where you had to strip off all your dirty clothes before you ran naked throught the house to your bathroom!)*

The next area of the house was her pantry, and of course, we knew groceries were destined for that pantry. It was part of the routine. It was normal. It was the natural order of life and things at the Smithsonian in my earliest years.

Little Jack and I knew very well that Friday was grocery store day. We also knew that at approximately 4 p.m. (you could almost set a watch to her Friday routine), my mother would come roaring across the dam between the ponds in front of our house toward the garage in her new yellow "T" Bird convertible, loaded with the week's groceries from the "Piggly Wiggly." *(I don't know just what those people were smoking when they named their business "Piggly Wiggly" but it was a great grocery store!)*

Little Jack and I devised an excellent plan. Using his unique "string poppers", We tied one end of the string to the inside door from the garage and the other end of the firecracker's string to the screen door. In fact, we thought this was such a great idea, we tied a whole box-full of these firecrackers to the door and the screen handle.

Friends, this was going to be a great event. This might even be a life changing situation for all of us.

Time was drawing near and we knew the yellow "T" Bird was due within minutes. We tied and tied and with our dastardly deed completed, we dashed out of the garage and into the nearby flower bed.

There was a wonderful window through the wall from which, we decided, would be the perfect position to watch the events unfold. Unfortunately, it was a little higher than we were able to reach on our tip toes, so we got bricks and built ourselves an official, military style "reviewing stand".

Ever on schedule, my mother left the highway for the drive across the dam. She was on two wheels when she made the right turn and floorboarded the "T" Bird. Of course her left foot was always on the brake (her brake lights never went out throughout her lifetime of driving automobiles) and she roared across the dam, hit the up-ramp into the garage at 40 miles an hour, as was her custom, simultaneously releasing the accelerator pressure while dramatically increasing the brake pressure, bringing the "T" Bird to a squawling halt only inches from the brick wall.

Eat Here & Get Gas!

As the "T" Bird rocked and attempted to settle itself, the driver's door flew open and in one motion, "Miss Martha" grabbed four Piggly Wiggly sacks (that's those brown paper sacks with a smiling, fat pig in an Army overseas cap on the side). She whirled around to her right executing a Ninja-style kick with her right foot to close the car door, and in two steps, grabbed the screen door handle with two fingers of her left hand as she carefully held jam packed Piggly Wiggly sacks full of groceries, and she snatched the screen door open...

Of course, Little Jack and I were perched on the brick reviewing stand just outside the garage window, watching the events unfold exactly as we had planned and just knew they would.

We were not only watching history in the making, we had our selves created it and we knew this was indeed a momentous occasion!

As you can imagine, when that screen door was snatched open and all those string poppers exploded, you would have thought both the Korean and Vietnam Conflicts were occurring in the Smithsonian Garage in Eastman, Georgia, all at the same time. It was incredible.

Get the picture here: The "T" Bird was still in motion, having not fully recovered as yet, and milk and eggs and lettuce and coffee and toilet paper and chocolate chips and napkins and tomatoes were everywhere in the air, all sailing in different directions. My mother was almost in suspended animation. I can still see the shock on her face even now as she reeled back through the air, groceries flying all about, her arms and legs gyrating, her eyes looking in all directions at the same time and she landed in the center of the garage...facing the window, trying to register exactly what was happening to her, only to see two deliriously-happy little faces totally engrossed in the successful outcome of their carefully planned mission.

We were howling without regard to the consequences; we instinctively knew something of real significance had occurred that day!

Needless to say, Little Jack was practically banned from *ever* visiting the Smithsonian again without adult supervision. If he did come, he was searched as he got out of his mother's car. He was relieved of his belt and suspenders;. Without which, his little hands would be constantly occupied holding up his pants thereby eliminating lots of opportunities for mischief.

Meanwhile, I was stripped of privileges, received swift and painful physical punishment and was barred from visiting Little Jack at his home or anywhere else forever.

Of course this only led Little Jack and me to develop other ways to harness our observational and planning skills, which we did much to our delight and punishment throughout our early school years.

As mean as that was, I have to tell you, the memory of my mother sailing through the air in our garage will forever be a most delightful and cherished episode of childhood!

Night Riders

"Charles, I'm going to have a talk with your mother."
Doris Frame

I think it was "Little Albert" who came up with the idea. Little Albert was Albert D. Glass, the second, the youngest son of A.D. Glass, Sr, one of the biggest landowners in Georgia and among the most eccentric people I have ever known, but that's another story.

Albert's idea was to get up in the middle of the night, get your parents car and steal away to meet your buddies and ride around for an hour or two.

Albert was one of my best friends growing up. He was almost exactly one year older than me and he was tough. His mother and dad were one of the regular couples my mother and dad enjoyed socializing with almost every night. Close friends up and down and all through the years even to this day.

Well, this all started when about a dozen or so boys in our age group organized into a "Get Your Parent's cars" group, quite informally of course.

Each Friday and/or Saturday night, beginning at about 1 in the morning, we would get out of bed, quietly make our way out of our homes, get into our parent's automobiles and drive to a predetermined meeting point, and then, the fun would begin.

Whether you drove your parent's car or you rode your bicycle to that rendezvous point didn't matter much. Of course, the really cool guys, drove cars. Understand, this was 1963. I was twelve years old. Albert was 13 and he was one of the oldest of the group.

Every Friday and Saturday night the group got bigger. We started out with four or five guys and the first thing you know, there were eight, nine, twelve people and more!

We would all crowd together in one or two cars and drive around for a couple of hours, come back to the rendezvous point, disband, and each one head for his own house, sneak back in, and none was the wiser. Parents didn't know anything had occurred.

Stealth was not a word we had heard at the time, but that was the order of the day. You had to operate in stealth to get the car out and back home, in my case, across a 300-yard dam between two ponds, lights off all the way, and safely back into the garage. 'Piece of cake!

Can you even imagine? I wouldn't do it now and it would actually be perfectly OK!

Friends, this was not a one-time event. It went on for months, and although there were no real incidents or accidents, I look back now and am thoroughly amazed. We just rode around,

Eat Here & Get Gas!

listening to the "Beatles" on WLS radio (can you believe it, that stands for "Worlds Largest Store." (It was an AM radio station broadcasting from Chicago and owned by Sears & Roebuck, the Worlds Largest Store!)

We would drive around, smoking cigarettes, usually Camels I got from my dad's supply or Parliaments Little Albert got from his mother, Miss Edith.

There were races, reckless driving, an occasional incident of running into a ditch, but no wrecks or any real physical damage. Of course, the night Bo Bo McCranie ran his dad's 59 Chevrolet Wagon into a ditch on a dirt road things were a little difficult. Some parts were torn off as we tried to drag it out of the ditch with a borrowed tractor but nothing much ever came of it.

One night, there was a crowd in my dad's 64 Ford Galaxie 500 with that powerful Police Interceptor engine. (He had ordered it for the Sheriff and had yet to deliver it) There were probably eight or more people in the car that night just driving around at 1:00 AM. We were headed through Eastman and passed the red-light at the Stuckey mansion.

As was ordinary, there was a young sailor standing there hitch-hicking. I slammed on brakes, the guys in the back opened the door, the sailor jumped in and we took off, almost as if it had been rehearsed. No problem.

As we sped out of the city, out past my home and toward the next little town, Gresston, GA, the sailor began to notice the young group he was riding with and asked me, the driver, **"How old are you?"**

"Twelve!" I responded proudly, and in sequence, every kid in the car responded with his age: Thirteen, twelve, eleven and-a-half, and so it went through the automobile.

By the time the last kid had responded, I noticed the sailor in the rear-view mirror and, you could tell, his color had changed completely. In fact, he had no color. Stark white, just like his uniform. He was visibly trembling!

Looking back, I'm not surprised, after all, he was in a speeding automobile at about two in the morning being driven by a twelve year old and the oldest person in the car was at least six years his junior. Of course, nobody had a driver's license.

Realizing he was scared to death, I locked the brakes and slid the car sideways into a rural grocery & gas station's parking area. As the car slid to a stop, in one motion, the boys in the back opened the door, pushed the sailor out, and we were once again headed south, all in a matter of seconds.

I always wondered what sort of stories that guy told about his fifteen minutes in a car-full of barely teenaged kids at two in the morning! I bet it was good. I would love to hear it!

Eat Here & Get Gas!

We never got caught in the entire time, more than a year! Close once or twice, but never caught.

The last time I was ever involved in the midnight rides, my friend David Frame, was spending the night at our house. We got permission to use my sister Pat's room, and even though we thought the pink walls and little girl decorations, and a pink and white tile bathroom were disgusting, we wanted that room because of the height of the bathroom window. It was easy access!

Midnight came around and we got up, snuck out and went to meet all the other guys. Great night. Drove for two hours and decided it was time to put the other guys out and head home. We didn't know one of the boy's mothers had gotten up and discovered him missing. We didn't know she had called the police.

Our task was just to get the car back across the dam, without lights, and get ourselves quietly back in the house, just like usual.

Creeping along ever so slowly to avoid driving the car into the ponds on either side of the driveway, we eventually made it right back to the same spot under the big pine tree just back from the two car garage. We parked what was my sister's car in her usual spot, switched off and were just about to get out of the car when I noticed a set of four headlights coming fast across the dam behind us. We ducked and waited for the car to come between our parking spot and the garage. Then we peeped up to see what was going on.

It was David's dad, Bill Frame. He looked upset and he stormed into our garage and was pressing what he thought was the doorbell.

Actually, it was a light switch that had originally been installed to be used to turn the lights inside the laundry room on from the garage, but I knew it had been disconnected.

Unfortunately, Mr. Frame thought he was ringing a doorbell when in fact he was ringing a light switch. Of course, I thought that was funny, 'cause he didn't know it wasn't a doorbell.

Well, friends, you ought not to laugh just because something is funny. There is a time and a place for everything, including laughing! This was not the time for laughter. It was what you call a big mistake.

Mr. Frame heard our laughter. He stormed the car, grabbed David by his right ear, pulled him out of the car and carried him to their car. David's feet didn't touch the ground twice. When they got into their automobile, a cream/white 1962 Mercury four door, they roared off, gravel and dust slung and stirred everywhere.

It took a few minutes, but, after the dust had settled, I didn't know exactly what to do.

I decided to sneak back through the window, get myself back in the bed in Pat's room, and just wait and see what might happen. I didn't know if

Eat Here & Get Gas!

my parents had heard all the commotion Mr. Frame had created. I was a little surprised that all the noise hadn't awakened my folks. Just lucky I guess! Could have been the Saturday night cocktails too I suppose!

About five-thirty the next morning, my dad woke me up and wanted to tell me he and my mother were going to drive over to Swainsboro to visit relatives. He said they wouldn't be back till late that afternoon.

He asked, "Where is David?"

I answered, quite honestly, *"He got sick and went home!"*

I know it wasn't the whole truth…but I also knew how true it really was.

Not 30 minutes after they were gone our telephone rang.

"Hello," I answered.

"Charles, this is Doris Frame." (David's mother). *"I want to speak to your mother this minute"*, she continued in her very upset yankee voice. "I'm going to tell her what you boys have been up to."

"She ain't here!" I responded.

"When will she be back."

"I'm not exactly sure Mrs. Frame," in my best, most innocent and charming voice. (Eddie Haskell could have learned quite a bit from me that morning!)

"Well, I'm going to tell her all about what you boys have been doing," and she hung up.

Charles M. Williams

Now there's a real pickle for you. I sat there the entire day, a beautiful Sunday at that, and stewed over what I should do. Eventually and quite painfully I arrived at what I considered the best conclusion: that as bad as it was, it would still be better if *I* told my parents instead of having them hear it first from a very angry Mrs. Doris Frame. I thought she might not tell them as softly as maybe I could, know what I mean?

Dutifully, that evening, when I could get up my courage, I did tell my mother and dad that, last night, David and I had driven the car across the dam and back and his mother and dad found out about it and they were really upset.

Well, sure, I knew it wasn't the whole thing. They interrogated me and got enough more that whatever was missing no longer mattered.

The punishment was swift, severe, and long-lasting. It included a long talk, a hairbrush, a belt, many additional chores, and weeks of walking from our house all the way to the elementary school, the other side of our community from my house. It was severe enough that I still remember it after all these years. Plus, it was indeed my last time taking the family cars out for a midnight spin.

The most interesting part was that to this day, Mrs. Frame has yet to call again…and it's been 40 years.

"Kennedy Half-Dollar!"

"Had it been another day, I might have looked the other way..."
"I've Just Seen a Face" Lenon-McCartney

I was 9 years old. I was a member in good standing of a wonderful loving family at a time of significant economic prosperity. The bulk of the Baby-Boom generation was just ahead of me and all the great planning, building, and expansion to accommodate that huge group of people was just about completed when I was in grade school.

There was more to come, of course, because we lived in the "rural South" and all the great things that happened in the rest of the country eventually made their way here after a few years. There was a lot to be said for living in the south though.

For example, all the noteworthy things the "boomers" did, like the hippie movement out in California, now that was the place I pictured as the absolute last resort for people in the USA, it just wasn't happening in the South. I figured early on that any person who couldn't hold on anywhere else in the country would eventually slide, as if in a funnel, all the way to California. Those who couldn't hold on there just slid on into the Pacific!

Charles M. Williams

I grew up with a very high opinion of Georgia, without regard to the fact that we were referred to by many as backward, crackers, rednecks, and poor deprived people of the land. I had already seen Mr. Stuckey make a fortune by selling "rubber alligators" to the Northerners headed for "Flair-i-duh", a state not much different from California, in my young (and my continued) opinion.

The two biggest differences were that Florida seemed to attract the older folks while California attracted the wild, young people.

Secondly, Florida was dangerously close to my beloved Georgia, while California was safely a continent's width away. Northerners, or Yankees as we called 'em, were only a half a continent out and above us, and I was never completely comfortable with that fact until I realized they had toll roads everywhere up there and I figured that was a pretty good barrier. I was good in geography as a kid in the early grades.

Of course, I knew there was the Sunshine Parkway, a Florida toll-road, but I figured that was the result of people from Minn-so-tuh and New-Yoowaak, and other Yankee lands moving south to avoid the cold weather. Surely no right thinking, genuine Southerner would come up with the idea for a toll-road. No way!

Our little Georgia community was organized along the old railroad lines in the early 1800s.

Eat Here & Get Gas!

Seems a couple of far-sighted Northerners, one named Dodge—William E. Dodge—and the other named Eastman—William Pitt Eastman—their parents seem to have had a "thing" for the name "William", and of course that fact was not lost on me, a Williams myself. In fact I believe everybody was originally named Williams. Fact is many of you have had to change your last name for one reason or the other. The pure among us are still Williamses!

Anyway, these northern businessmen recognized the huge stores of virgin pine timber in our area of central Georgia. They financed and built rail lines into the heart of this part of the state to haul the mighty timbers back up north. Tram lines were built that extended out from the main rail lines. Local people were hired to cut the timber and drag it to the tram lines with oxen and mules where it was loaded onto the flat cars and pulled to the main lines for transport north.

The profits *had* to be extensive. It costs money to build rail and tram lines, but with the timber virtually free for the taking and the labor available for what was likely a fraction of the existing northern standards, Eastman and Dodge were headed for the big time.

Funny, our county was named after Mr. Dodge and our county seat town is called Eastman. I always thought it had to do with Kodak color pictures, but that was another group of Eastmans!

Charles M. Williams

The trains still run through this community. These days, they don't slow down much unless they have just taken on a load at one of the local mills and haven't yet picked up a "head of steam" by the time they make downtown. Usually, they breeze through at something approaching 55 miles an hour. That's roaring for a train in a small community. I hope the "caution arms and signals" always work effectively. Trains can't stop even if they wanted to, you know!

Folks in the South have a way of saying someone isn't the sharpest pencil in the box when we use train warning signs to describe such a person. It goes like this: "Well, the lights is flashin', the bells is ringin', and the arms is comin' down, but they ain't no train!" Northerners would probably just say, "Duhhhh!" Bless their hearts!

Being a normally inquisitive kid with not too much to do on a weekday afternoon after school, I hung around the "Dixie-land" store. That was a local "five & dime" right in the middle of town facing the railroad tracks.

Of course, the town has since progressed and expanded away from the tracks. But in those days, that was the "downtown" area and it was where everything including the post office and another "dime" store. (I always wondered why they called them dime stores, because nothing in there was a dime, even when I was a boy.)

Eat Here & Get Gas!

There were then and still are today drug stores where you can get a real soda fountain Coke. (We were on cloud nine when the "soda-jerk" squirted either vanilla or cherry syrup in a Coke...way before today's "prefabricated" "canned" concoctions).

You couldn't help but love our little community. People knew other people forever. They might not know everyone individually, but you could bet they knew your daddy, your grandmother, or somebody who was your relative, and probably theirs!

On that particular day in "Dixie-Land", I was experimenting. There were two older ladies at the cash registers up near the doors and I wondered how sharp they were and how much attention they paid to their customers' purchases.

Dixie-Land was a very popular place and this was the middle to latter part of August when school supplies were in great demand. Lines formed at the checkout counters and I could see the ladies were very busy.

I thought it would be fun to remove the price tags from the $5 three-ring binders and also from the $1 binders, and then exchange them, just to see if the ladies at the cash registers would notice the difference.

Lines of people waited to be checked out. It was hot. The only semblance of air conditioning was a ceiling fan that pushed the ever-hotter air from the 10 foot ceiling down on the hot-enough air around the cash registers and already-sweaty customers!

There was nothing cool about it, just movement. But in those days, folks didn't think much about it and just enjoyed the breeze!

Those ladies worked at a fever pitch and I stood back about three aisles away, watching carefully as the "changed" notebooks were about to be presented to the cashier by an unsuspecting young customer. 'Fourth in line, third, moments away when a flash of red caught my eye from three aisles and a cash register away.

Outside the store, walking along with her boyfriend was the cutest little blond-haired girl in a bright red outfit. The unsuspecting young customer was second in line, but my attention was redirected. I wanted to see the cashier's reaction, but the sight outside the store windows had me totally distracted and I left my post at aisle four and dashed outside to get another glimpse at this pretty little blonde.

She was 9 years old! Her boyfriend was one of my best friends, Joel Whigam, whose dad was the postmaster in Eastman. She was from Chauncey. Her name was Charlotte. That's all the information I had at the time, but I knew without the slightest doubt from my very first glance, in my 9-year-old brain, she was special. I just couldn't stop thinking about her, *(and still haven't more than 40 years later.)*

Eat Here & Get Gas!

I told my seventh-grade homeroom teacher, Miss Alma Cannon, that Charlotte and I were going to get married. She made a 50 cent bet with me that by high school, I would be dating someone else.

One year after we married, June 1971, I received a sweet card with a Kennedy half-dollar glued inside. It is one of my most favorite keepsakes!

Charlotte has, for nearly four decades, two grown sons, and many experiences later, been my best friend and most delightful companion. I am so glad to tell you she still is the one for me!

By the way, the Dixie-land cashiers were very sharp. They caught my mischief and corrected the mistake on the spot. From that time forward they seemed to watch me more carefully anytime I was in their store.

How sad it is to me that so many people these days leave their wives and husbands because "he got ugly" or "she got fat" or the "kids are a real pain" or the ever popular "I just want someone better, more exciting" and on and on and on!

People need to stop and think. Who is perfect? Who hasn't gained weight? Who hasn't gotten older? Who doesn't have "baggage" to carry along to the next "more perfect" possibility? Who can you meet that fits any of those criteria. They don't exist!

Charles M. Williams

Whatever happened to the "NO RETURN/NO REFUND" policy that was and should still be an integral part of the marriage contract?

You make a marriage work by working at it! Two people, committed to the success of a marriage can make a marriage successful. No other formula works.

God knows I am both fat and ugly and difficult to live with. Charlotte, on the other hand, just gets better and better, and you know what, I make it a point to tell her that every day, even on those days when for whatever reason, I might not be totally convinced.

I encourage her to keep it up. I give her something to live up to. She does the same for me. We do the same thing together for our children. We try to do the same thing for people with whom we come in contact.

Neither of us is anywhere near perfect, but we are a perfect match. Because we work at it.

Seems too many people just get tired or bored or disenchanted.

"The grass is always greener" concept seems to come into play, but one thing you can count on with grass, friends; no matter where it is, you still have to mow it!

That old Dixie-land store has long since closed as a five-and-dime. The building is still there and today, it is run by another dear friend of mine, Miss Juanita Pittman. It is a print shop and office

Eat Here & Get Gas!

supply center and I make it a point to go in there and buy things every time I can. It's still fun to go in and stand around looking out the window toward the railroad tracks! There are lots of wonderful memories in that old store for me! In fact, every now and then, I can still catch a quick glimpse of bright Red flashing by the window headed for College Street Pharmacy for a vanilla coke on crushed ice.

A Wing Tip Shoe

Her dream school. It was a magical place...many of us still visit.
CMW

I firmly believe that if all my teachers had been like my sixth-grade teacher, Mrs. Merle Bennett, I would have been a brain surgeon. She was tough. She was hard. She was demanding and she was absolutely determined that her students would waste no time, spare no effort, and miss no opportunity to stretch themselves to reach her goals. When you walked into her classroom, you sat down, got out a book, and promptly went to work. "Miss Bennett was tough just like "Miss Jones" and "Miss Ragan" and all my teachers up to that point in my education. Things were about to change!

With seventh grade and no longer staying with the same teacher all day all year, new experiences were just ahead.

"Miss Clyde" was one of the biggest changes I guess I had ever seen up until that time. "Miss Clyde" was old. In fact, "Miss Clyde" had been in her mid 40s when she taught my *mother* and in her *70s* when she taught my sister. The wonderful story of her dream school was a predominant subject in practically every class she ever taught. It was something to behold!

By the time I made it to her seventh-grade English class, as you might well imagine, she was ancient. "Miss Clyde" or more formally, Mrs. Clyde Burch, was the consummate Southern English teacher. Diagramming sentences on the blackboard, correcting our verb tenses and spelling were her forte'. Tedious, thankless work that is as much a part of a fundamental education as there is, and "Miss Clyde" was good at it. She spent hours telling us about her marvelous, highly futuristic dream school. You couldn't help enjoying her imagination. 'Probably made a huge contribution toward encouraging my own!

Seventh and eighth grade classrooms were in the "old building". There was a clock tower, an old auditorium, and a crawl space under the old wooden floors that lots of seventh and eight graders actually stood up in! What an exciting place and time!

Of course, going under the building was strictly prohibited, which is why it was absolutely essential to go there. Quite by accident, one of the very best ways to access the forbidden space was from Miss Clyde's coat closet, more fondly referred to as the cloak room!

As the founder of the proverbial "old school," Miss Clyde rendered punishments for various infractions, such as chewing gum, belching, and a

Eat Here & Get Gas!

host of other seventh-grade crimes, and her usual sentence was suspension into the cloak room! Imagine that!

"Please, oh please, don't throw me in the Briar Patch!"

Every day, somebody, usually Billy Ray, another of those delightful southern two-first named boys, was banished to the cloak room for whatever impropriety he had committed on that particular occasion. And, as so many generations before him, he would immediately remove the books from the bottom shelf and slip through the hole in the age-old plaster and into the magical and enticing crawl space under the building.

Joy. Freedom. Power. Cigarettes. Matches. Ahhh. Much better than class anytime, and practically every participant through the ages agreed!

People who where being punished could indeed climb up as well as down from the cloak room. If they we're really industrious, they could reach the old clock tower and maybe even be lucky enough to catch a pigeon. *The natural dangers present in a very old structure should have been enough to curb our appetites for adventure. The added sensation that Mr. Casteel's, our principal, punishment would be quite severe if caught in any of these areas should have crystalized our judgement to prevent us from being here. However, the joy of innocence, the sense of adventure, and the testosterone flowing in the veins of twelve year old boys was simply overwhelming.*

On one such excursion under the building, Billy Ray found an old wingtip shoe, probably a size-12 with quite a bit of wear and decades of dust. The shoe, no doubt, had an interesting history and an excellent reason for being under the building. On this day, it was recovered by Billy Ray on one of his many excursions under the building and resurrected to the light of day in Miss Clyde's classroom, much to the delight of all the other cloak room inhabitants and fellow underworld partners.

It was always humorous to me that Miss Clyde never seemed to realize that from a student's perspective, the cloak room represented *opportunity,* not punishment. She either feigned ignorance, or just didn't notice all the objects, such as the wingtip shoe, hammer handles, or the various and sundry items that appeared in her English class from time to time. Looking back, I'm sure age had its effect, however, she might well have been intentionally creating memories. Either way, the results were positive!

One morning, about half-way through the seventh grade, Viola was a bit ticked with me for whatever it is that seventh-grade girls get upset

Eat Here & Get Gas!

with seventh-grade boys over. She *pretended* to trip over my outstretched legs as she returned to her desk from the pencil sharpener. Viola was a vision of loveliness. We were distantly related and found that to be a problem, since we really liked each other, but it was not to be.

Whether I actually intended to trip her or not, it was a calculated gamble on Viola's part to enlist Miss Clyde's assistance to obtain revenge for whatever I did to deserve that morning's outrage. Believe me, it was effective.

Miss Clyde went ballistic, if a woman of her age and limited physical range was actually still able to do that. She couldn't locate her paddle, imagine that, however, finding that old shoe, she used it as a pretty good substitute and proceeded to wear me out right then and there, dust, flapping leather sole and all, and then immediately sent me out to <u>stand in the hall</u>.

Now, standing in the hall in and of itself wasn't all that bad. I got to know the janitors pretty well and heard lots of things taking place in other classrooms. The inherent danger however was several-fold: First, I got behind in whatever was going on in class. Not too big a deal here, but all the same, there could be serious consequences.

Second: Some other teacher that you didn't want to get to know, like, Mr. Coley for instance, just might happen by and invite me down to his hall for a visit with his "Board of Education." No one wanted that although occasionally, I could hear the sounds of others being introduced to the Coley Board through the reverberating echos of the old wooden walls and the high ceilings. On those occasions, the entire school would sit up and take notice. Very effective communication indeed! You can say corporal punishment is not effective but I can guarantee you, after you heard a serious "Board Meeting" going on in those ancient, highly resonant hallways, you can bet every kid in school got a little twinge in his rear, not unlike the calming effect a State Trooper vehicle brings to every driver breezing down an interstate highway…you know exactly what I mean.

Finally, and I guess worst of all, Mr. Casteel just might have found me in the hall as he made his rounds. He was the principal of the school and was rumored to have had an electric paddle, the terror of the seventh grade.

Billy Ray had been sent to Mr. Casteel's office many times and invariably returned to boggle our young minds with tales of the terrifying electric paddle.

All of us, especially this little fat seventh-grader, dreaded even the thought of such a device.

The dread of the punishment itself was almost as much as the fact that such an encounter would immediately be relayed directly to my parents by the teachers working undercover for them in the

Eat Here & Get Gas!

school. Without question, no one wanted Mr. Casteel to find them in the hall, and thanks to Viola, here I was, again.

In a matter of moments, I heard his sharp shoe heels as they clipped and clapped over the polished tile floors as he made his rounds. The dread of the ages was on my mind as the footsteps neared and I had no place to hide.

Thankfully I had befriended the janitors. I brought my dad's cigarettes and such things as presents, and quickly found my way into the back of the broom closet long enough for Mr. Casteel to vanish 'round the corner and down the eighth-grade hall.

Then, with only seconds to spare, I quickly and quietly returned to my punishment post, outside Miss Clyde's classroom door, only an instant before she came to the door to ask me if I could "behave" if she let me back in.

Disaster of the day just barely avoided I responded, "Of course," and I enthusiastically and contritely agreed. Once resettled in my desk and after receiving a sly smile from Viola, I proceeded to plan a similar fate for her in the near future. I could only hope she would not be so fortunate and resourceful as I had been on this outing!

And so it went throughout grade school. Lifelong memories and friendships were begun and many have continued to this day.

Charles M. Williams

Although everyone pretty much lost track of Billy Ray. I know he quit school in the eighth grade, found himself a job, went to work and to my knowledge, simply vanished.

Nevertheless, my memories of and inspiration from him live on all these years later. He was a dare-devil. He smoked cigarettes. He wasn't afraid of any teacher, coach, or principal. He was the first "rebel" I ever actually remember in my first hand experience. Of course, he was four years older than the rest of us and he had been in the same grade for several of those years. That might have been a part of his rebellion, but, wherever it came from, I remember it. Best of all, I remember that old shoe he found and brought in from his visit to the Cloakroom and the fun I've had sharing that story ever since.

The Tooth-Dentist

Hardly any childhood memory compares with '50s Dentistry!
CMW

Those of us born in the late 1940s or early 1950s shared a common experience. The world was a prosperous place then. There was this brand new thing called TV. It was exciting. Anything that was not just right was being either being replaced with something NEW or being vastly IMPROVED.

We heard it all the time on TV, you know, *"New and Improved!"* I Always wondered: If something is actually "NEW" how could it at the same time be "IMPROVED?" But such is television.

Walter Cronkite and Douglas Edwards were becoming household names. There were jet aircraft and the most fortunate among us might have even seen a helicopter first-hand.

Schwinn Corvette bikes were the rage! Those were heady times. Cars had big, beautiful fins. Some had push-button gear shifters, swivel seats and even *real* record players. "Davey, Davey Crocket, k-k-k-k-king of the wild frontier" Played and stuttered over the little car speaker. The stutter was usually the result of a bump in the road. It was a far cry from today's CD players,

DVD Players, and the whole digital phenomenon, but it was popular and "leading edge" at the time!

'No doubt it was a time of great change for all of us. However, the one place where time seemed just to stand still in my young world was at the dentist's office.

There were 26 steps from the street level up to Dr. Harrell's office. I knew it was supposed to be a simple check-up. I knew I would get to see "Miss Helen," she was Dr. Harrell's wife, dental assistant, and sweet, sweet child settler-downer. I loved her every day of her life, although I believe I could always detect a slight scent of novacaine anytime I hugged her neck.

Air conditioning hadn't made it to the top floor dentist's office back then. (In fact, it never did). I was scheduled for a visit to the dentist's office. I was not pleased with the idea, however, my mother was strong, purposeful and merciless. That woman had a look she could send across a room that would absolutely immobilize a child, especially one of her own young 'uns!

Dr. Harrell's office had open windows with a view of the 40 plus year-old built-up tar roof of the adjoining building. I had already been in the waiting room that overlooked Main Street and was totally keyed up for the *"aaaahhhhhhhhhhiiiiiiiieeeeeee"* that regularly came about two minutes into the part where Dr. Harrell would be drilling into some poor soul's tooth.

Eat Here & Get Gas!

"whirrrrrrRRRRRRRRRRRGGGGGGGGGGGGGG GGGGGGGGGGGGGG" was the awful sound of that old belt-driven drill. I knew somebody was having a tooth filled and the drill had made it's way past the enamel, down through the decay, thoroughly penetrated the novacaine, and found its way, true to form, to *the nerve*.

Dr. Harrell seemed to have a highly polished (pardon the pun) knack for knowing just where that nerve was and invariably, he found it, usually when the drill changed from the *"RRRRRRRRRRRRRRR"* sound to the *"GGGGGGGGGGGGGG"* noise.

As I recall and write about that experience more than four decades later, there is a distinct tingling in my lower jaw even today.

I thought Dr. Harrell was a very old man. He was likely in his late '40s about then and, to a young kid, that was ancient and near death. He had greying hair. He was skinny and small. His hands had a certain unsteadiness about them. Of course it was exaggerated when discussed among siblings and friends who had experienced what was actually very good dental care at his hands...such is the stuff of legends you know!

I remember the first time Dr. Harrell decided I had a cavity that needed to be filled. Friends, when he came at me with that three foot-long needle to "deaden" my gums (I know it wasn't really three feet-long, but it was huge and memory makes it ever larger all these years later) my gum was anything but "deadened". That novacaine might well have decreased the sensitivity in the half-inch square area it touched, but every other nerve in my body doubly over-compensated.

Sweat streamed out of every pore in my skin. Just the very thought of climbing those stairs, let alone watching that huge shot headed for my mouth was an awful experience grown ever larger through the passing of time.

His hands shook and he smiled and said, "naw, this won't hurt much, just a little." I remember hearing that awful, piercing "aaaahhhhh-hhhhiiiiiiieeeeeee" sound, and not even realizing it was coming from me.

"Just a little. Might sting some! Won't hurt much. Huuuuuuuuhhhhh?

Every cell in my body energized and I struggled to get out of that chair. My total focus was on the tarred rooftop just outside the window facing his upstairs office. Of course he always stood between me and the window; he had this huge hypodermic needle filled with novacaine in his right hand, and Miss Helen stood there with an "I-understand-Huuuuney" smile she was using to the best of her ability to hold me back.

And there was my mother, standing just to the side of the chair with that *look*...I know you've seen a similar look, the one that, if said, would have sounded like "If you think this is painful, you

Eat Here & Get Gas!

just wait 'till I get you home and tell your daddy how you embarrassed me and our entire family at the dentist's office. He's going to pull off body parts and beat you senseless with them."

You would have to hear her tell it in person to get the truly hilarious effect, but Mimi (Daniels) Dennis, the daughter of Marsden and Nanny Daniels, dear friends of our family, becomes excitingly animated when she recalls one of her childhood visits to Dr. Harrell. Of course, Mimi is animated, regardless the subject. That's a big part of her vibrant personality. However, nowhere is she more delightful than in tellng this story about having her teeth cleaned in Dr. Harrell's office.

Mimi goes into great detail, arms swinging, eyes sparkling, and that impish smile she gets when she's into her story. I can remember her telling me:

"There wasn't a problem. The drill made its usual noises and as always it was uncomfortable and hot." She started laughing and said, "You know how the dentist's head is always *reeeaaaal* close to your head when he is working inside your mouth? "Well" pronounced "Waa-yulll" (one of her favorite words) Well, I was just looking at his glasses 'sorta watching the reflection of him cleaning my teeth. You know, just watching what he was doing in there, when all of a sudden, his glasses were covered with a spray of blood.

I didn't even realize it was my blood! There was no pain, just a sudden spray that covered his glasses.

Apparently, the rubber tip used for cleaning had gotten a bit close to my lip and caused it to open up with a spraying motion. I screamed. Dr. Harrell was shocked. We both were taken aback. It took a few minutes to get settled back down, glasses cleaned, and my fingernails out of the ceiling. I will never forget the look on his face, blood splattered glasses and all!"

Naturally, Mimi shared her experience with other people and embellished it for each group of listeners in the true, Southern fashion. Nothing bad, just one-ups-man ship of the highest order. Ain't one been born better than Mimi at embellishing a story and making you a living part of it, unless maybe it is her mom, Miss Nanny!

Over the years, it seems Mimi and I often have the same regularly scheduled check-up dates at our current dentist's office. Invariably, we share 'horror stories' from days gone by and she never fails to make me cry with laughter when she gyrates through that event once again.

In addition to excellent dental services and education, I think one of the by products of Dr. Harrell's practice was totally unintentional but every bit effective:

Eat Here & Get Gas!

I don't think any of the people of our generation who visited Dr. Harrell had any problem with the concept of **Hell** in church.

When bother Max O'Neal talked about eternal damnation, I clearly saw Dr. Harrell and his shots and heard that awful "whirrrrrr-RRRRRRRRRRR—GGGGGGGGGGGGGGGGGGGGGGGGGGG" and could feel him nervously and forever filling my teeth.

Trust me! I wanted to be good! Whatever it took, I wanted to be good! I understood eternal punishment. I could see, feel and taste it!

Dentistry has improved dramatically in my lifetime and I am very thankful for that fact. Laughing gas, elevator music, quiet drilling equipment, more serene surroundings. Without question it is much improved. Dr. Smith is as gentle as any dentist could possibly be.

However, my fears and distant memories are covered with the thinnest of skins (and the rawest of nerves). Dr. Harrell did more to encourage excellent behavior on my part than anybody else I can remember! *I can tell you, that man made a believer out of me!*

Wakin' up is hard to do!

This is as true a story as I have ever made up in my life.
CMW

Like most Southerners, the majority of my family members attended the Baptist Church every Sunday morning in my growing-up years. Not just any Baptist Church, mind you, but the *FIRST* Baptist Church.

I correctly say majority because "Mommer and the young-'uns" was going, which was always four out of five family members, even though I noticed daddy only went around Christmas and Easter.

Even then it was 'cause Momma would put up such a hissey-fit. I used to wonder what the preacher meant at the Christmas service when he would wish everybody there a Happy Easter, and again at the Easter Service when he would wish everyone a Merry Christmas, but, I guess that was really the only time he saw lots of those people and he wanted them to feel welcome.

Every Sunday morning was the same as the next at our house. We got to sleep a little later since my mother usually didn't wake us up with the vacuum cleaner on Sunday. "Ought not to work on the Lord's day, you know," so sleeping until around 7:30 am was usually acceptable. Sunday school started at 10:00, preaching at 11:00. Brother Max was armed and dangerous. He could run the devil out of whatever corners he might be hiding in!

My mother came into the room my brother and I shared and proceeded to wake us up. She told us breakfast would be ready in 15 minutes and that we should get up and get dressed for Sunday School. It didn't take me long to realize I only needed 15 minutes, flat, start to finish, to be all dressed and ready to go. Why she thought two hours were required was beyond me but, invariably, she started the process promptly at 7:30 a.m.

She was providing the same wake-up service for my brother at the same time, but he always chose to just ignore it on Sunday, even more astutely than on the regular weekdays.

I was always amazed that no wake-up call was ever provided or needed on Saturday mornings when there was no school, no Sunday school, and no nothing! Getting up was never a problem for me, particularly on Saturdays when my mother's vacuum roared.

On Sunday, mornings I crawled out of bed, took care of business, got dressed and "reported" to the kitchen to smell the bacon frying and to watch my daddy smoke Camel cigarettes and drink black coffee.

My mother happily prepared a meal for her family and the ceramic tile on the kitchen floor was always cool to my feet. It was the calm before the routine Sunday storms.

"Is your brother up?" she invariably asked on Sunday mornings when I arrived in the kitchen as required.

"No M'am!" was my regular and honest response. Same thing different week.

"Go get him up and tell him breakfast will be ready in five minutes," was always her next, thoroughly predictable statement.

"But, he's gonna'..."

"You go get him. Tell him *I* said to get up and come to breakfast, RIGHT NOW!"

"Yessum! (good Southern word)" and here we'd go again.

Of course, I knew my brother didn't plan to get up.

I knew that my mother *knew* that my brother had no intention of following the "rules".

Absolutely, I knew the eventual outcome of this process would result in my mother appearing in our bedroom with a snarl and a hairbrush and that I would be the intended target of her aggression since I would have done something I shouldn't have to my brother.

I also knew that whatever I did to get him out of bed was going to infuriate him and that there would be pushing and shoving and a lick or two passed between us. It was a regularly scheduled program of events. It happened practically every Sunday morning of our growing up years.

Most of all, I knew, and I knew that she knew, that all this was just ahead.

I would be sent on a mission to get the boy out of his bed.

Creativity, could've been mischief, clicked in. I figured I might as well have fun in the process.

Understand, I *knew* I was going to wind up with a beating, whatever I did, however I handled the situation, regardless!

So, every Sunday I came up with yet another way to get the boy out of bed. 'Couldn't be a weekday plan, 'had to be a Sunday special, you know, like cold wet towels or putting a handful of pepper under his nose, or any creative, effective, method I could dream up. None of this normal, "get-up-stuff" worked anyway. So, creativity clicked in. In fact, I thrived on it!

Naturally, my brother would come out fighting. Fist fights meant broken bedboards, destroyed chairs, broken lamps and damage to virtually everypiece of furniture and everything else that was in our part of the "Smithsonian!" (my friends name for my mother's immaculate and well appointed house).

Back to the story: Shortly after the fight would get underway, my mother would come in squalling and yelling and swinging her belt or hairbrush or bacon fork.

Eat Here & Get Gas!

I always went out with little red lashes on my legs and back from whatever she happened to have had in her hands. Then I went back to the kitchen and waited and listened for things to settle down in the bedroom while my daddy enjoyed his Sunday paper, black coffee, and Camels. It was a natural ebb and flow like the seasons. It just happened every week on Sunday mornings. It was life at its normal, steady pace for me.

One particular Sunday morning, the routine began as usual. I reported to the kitchen as trained. I was dressed and ready for the events to unfold. I knew what was coming. I dreaded it, but, with something of a mischievous mind, at the same time, I looked forward to it. There is a certain comfort to a routine you know, almost without regard to the routine itself.

"Go get your brother up!" came the command from my mother.

Understand, I had been in this routine for some time now and had become rather comfortable with the process. In fact, I had planned that particular Sunday's events for several weeks and had conjured up what I knew would be the *wake-up call to end all wake-up calls!*

Everything was set. Daddy enjoyed the steps unfolding before him, a circle of Camel smoke surrounding his newspaper. It was neither Christmas or Easter so he wasn't thinking of getting ready for church. No hurry!

Charles M. Williams

Of course, he had to side with my mother when she got really upset, but, no doubt in my mind, he knew something was up for the day and he was enjoying the show!

"Go get your brother up!" Momma repeated, pointing her dripping bacon fork in my direction.

Down the two steps into the living room from the kitchen, around the furniture, up the two steps at the other end of the room up to the hall, past the library on the right, that's where the piano was, and past the guest bedroom on the left, down the hall on the left past my sister's pink room, parent's room was straight ahead. On my right was the door to the room my brother and I shared.

My bed was the first on the left, his was next. And there he was friends and neighbors, snoring, unsuspecting, and yet, fully prepared for the events about to unfold.

Understand, I had previously tried all sorts of concoctions with varying degrees of wake-up success. Yet, on this particular morning, a simpler more direct tactic was in order. As usual, my brother slept on his stomach, with his left arm hanging down the side of the bed and his fingers dangling within inches of the floor.

I estimated a Webster's dictionary was about the thickness I needed to accomplish my mission and I had one of the perfect size and dimension in my closet.

Eat Here & Get Gas!

With this wonderful book in place, I slid a bowl of pleasantly warm water on top of the book, just perfect for his dangling fingers to be submerged.

A full night's rest generally leaves one's bladder at capacity by morning wake-up time, and since I knew normal wake-up had already passed, I surmised correctly, relying on my elementary science education and discussions with friends and associates and fellow conspirators, that a sleeping person's fingers resting in warm water can readily stimulate a bladder's total and involuntary release.

With everything expertly in place and the world of science about to come to life, I deftly removed myself from the immediate area and quietly observed from the safety of the hallway.

Dear reader, science worked beyond my wildest expectations only *much* more quickly and thoroughly than I had ever anticipated.

While my saturated brother left the room for the adjoining restroom and bath area in search of dry clothing and secrecy for what had happened, I quietly and with great agility removed the dictionary, the bowl, and all other evidence.

I learned two extremely valuable lessons that have lasted a lifetime:

First, there are many ways to accomplish your objectives in this old world without resorting to physical confrontations;

Charles M. Williams

Second and most important, a little creativity goes a long way. You see, a little dampness in one's bed at the appropriate place and time will cause a rapid wake-up, get-up and get going sequence.

Why, I believe, done correctly, it can be placed there by some other person, and the victim will indeed believe it to be of his or her own making.

The Sunday morning fights quietly ended after that incident and breakfast has been my best favorite meal ever since!

"What did the Preacher Preach about this mornin' son?"

Why is it that nothin' is ever as funny anywhere else as it is in Church
'Most ALL of us

My mother had great faith and placed much stock in appearances. If you looked like you were doing well, and you felt like you were doing well, then, by golly, you were doing well!

I always figured Sunday mornings were set aside for appearances. My mother, older sister, brother and I were trotted off to church all dressed up in our Sunday clothes (there was a real difference between Sunday clothes and other clothes) loaded up in the car, and drove to the First Baptist Church.

"Stop that whimpering! Dry your eyes! You'll mess up your shirt! Tighten that tie…" These were the admonishments my mother offered as my sister of 15 stressfully practiced her driving.

My mother read her Sunday School lesson and touched up her nails on the way to church. My brother and I tried to figure out quiet ways to torture each other in the back seat. We knew better than to get caught *again.* That might take away the tremendous freedom of not having to sit by our dear mother during the church service. That woman could look at you hard enough to make your blood thin and she could pinch you with a measured pain that was easily enough to stop your breathing, but just under the threshold for releasing a church-wide scream.

Needless to say, we didn't want to have to sit with her in church. That was in fact the longest hour in any kid's lifetime. I figured out pretty quickly that I had to demonstrate to her that I would behave, even if I wasn't by her side during the service. That would mean I could earn the right to sit *anywhere* else.

I think my mother always enjoyed showing off her children. I think that is a natural phenomenon and occurs in every part of the country. I think it is especially important in the small-town South. 'Ain't much else to show off here, I suppose and if that's the way it is, so be it!

As a result, my sister's dresses were always bright, fluffy, and lacy. Her hair was always "just so" with the right ribbons, the right shiny shoes, you get the picture.

I can remember "church ladies" coming up to us and saying, "Oh Martha, your Pat is just so beautiful, and those *young men* are *so* handsome!"

Can you imagine what that sounded like to an aggressive young boy?

Eat Here & Get Gas!

    The last thing I ever wanted to hear was that I was handsome! My hair was so greased down and my skin was so scrubbed that by the time I got to church, I felt a need to slide some of the grease down off my hair and rub it in my face just to get the skin to loosen up a bit.

    I sat absolutely, perfectly still under the threat of losing my Sunday afternoon outdoor privileges, I was barely allowed to look around in church. It didn't take long to get the preacher's messages: *Do right. Bring money.*

    I figured out the messages came in all kinds of stories and pictures and phrases and sermons, but it was basically the same message week after week–come to think of it, 'can't say it's changed much in my lifetime.

    My imagination clicked in and helped me pass those agonizing hours at my mother's side. In our church, there is a wonderful balcony. I longed for the day I could leave my mother's side and sit up there away from everyone, mostly her.

    Shortly after services began, I readily recognized the day's message as a creative rerun of all the others. I would look up toward the ceiling at the huge lights suspended on long cables over the congregation. I suppose I had been watching too many *Tarzan* and other Disney and adventure movies. I could actually see myself standing on the edge of the balcony. There I was, towering above the people below and, donning my Zorro cape (you couldn't be in church with only a *Tarzan* loin cloth you know). Holding the cable from the center light in my right hand, my genuine Walt Disney-Zorro sword in hand, swinging down from the balcony toward the pulpit where the preacher was at the height of his message.

I locked my legs around his chest and with the momentum of the arc as the cable swung from the light fixture carrying us both up over the choir loft and higher still to the waiting baptismal pit, I released my grasp of the cable. This sent me with the wailing preacher out of sight through the curtains, down into the water and away to freedom.

Naturally, this creative entertainment and dynamic action was much to the delight and cheers of the congregation who would stand up and cheer.

I could hear their grateful applause of the resourcefulness of this bright, young "Zorro-Zan" who saved them from any more of the sermon.

I could hear the cheering in my mind as clearly as if it were actually occurring, and was always a little shocked when my imagination would be jarred back to the reality of the situation and I would realize, I had in fact never left my mother's side. All that wonderful cheering I thought was for me was actually the congregation standing to sing the "Hymn of Invitation" ('never quite figured out why they called it *invitation*...I thought it ought to be called the "Go-Home Hymn"!)

'No matter! My imagination served me well! Zorro-Zan has been with me in every church service I ever sat through. Sometimes I swung on vines, sometimes from a rope suspended from a helicopter. Hydraulic doors could open and swallow up a preacher at the loudest portion of his message. Scuba divers could come along and cart him away underwater with dispatch. Imagination was an amazing space then and it still works!

When we would finally get home, Daddy was usually there, often grilling a chicken on the patio and having another Camel. He always jokingly asked, "What did the preacher preach about?" I knew the answer he expected. It was always the same.

"**Sin!**" I responded.

"What did he say about it?" he would follow-up with a little wry smile."

"It was **bad**!" I responded!

We would both laugh, being careful not to let "Miss Martha" hear us; she sorta' took all that personal you know, appearances as they wuz!

Gaining my mother's eventual confidence and not having to report to her after Sunday School for an hour of perfect stillness and painful threats is among my greatest memories of church as a young boy. It was a right of passage if you will. I was elated to sit anywhere but by her side. Oh what a delightful feeling of relief not to sit there within either her eyeshot or her grasp. It was powerful training. Powerful!

It took years before I was able to sit anywhere other than with my mother. Years! It was my image of what a stern judge's sentence would be.

Eventually, I was allowed to venture out a few rows ahead of her, then to the center section of pews, then all the way to the other side of the church. Eventually, I was allowed to venture all the way up to the much coveted balcony.

It was there in that balcony one Sunday morning I was introduced to a universal truth: *The things that happen in church are 1,000 times funnier than the same things happening anywhere else.*

I was about to learn that truth, the *hard* way.

I sat along side my older brother and his friend, Russell. In fact, I was next to the huge air conditioning unit, Russell was next to me and then Verne, sat next to Russell. (Yes, *Verne* is his *real* name).

Like other kids who look for quiet activities that could occupy our minds during those long services (they seemed interminable to me and I guess other kids, and some adults), Russell sketched in his hymnal.

He was working pretty hard and I knew he was a good artist. I thought it was a bit odd that he was actually drawing in the front cover of the hymnal, but I reasoned he didn't have any paper other than that, so I figured it was OK.

Now, just about halfway through that sermon, when Brother Max was genuinely getting into his rhythm, Russell decided it was time to let me have a full, first-hand look at his masterpiece on which he had been working so hard.

Ya'll, right there in front of me, on the hard, inside front cover of the Baptist hymnal, in beautiful, permanent, indelible, black "Bic" pen, from the hands and eyes of a talented, creative-if-somewhat misdirected-and-overly-productive young mind, was one of the clearest, most detailed pictures of Satan himself I have ever seen, period.

I can see it this minute as if it were right in front of me. The image faced left, had smooth, sharp pointed horns protruding from the forehead. Mean, dark eyes shining with the most unforgettable, devious little half-smile, half-sneer I have *ever* seen.

I know that when you're in a situation where laughing is not tolerated, anything remotely humorous will demand the heartiest laughter; Holding it back just makes the situation all the worse. It is just human nature. We've all been in that shape.

That picture of that devil in a Baptist hymnal at that particular time to a very young mind still ranks as one of the most hilarious things I have *ever* seen.

Ya'll, I burst out in an uncontrollable howl of laughter that immediately turned every head in the balcony my way, but it went further. Much further.

I couldn't see them, but I knew all the heads below were straining upward to see what in Heaven's name had caused such an irreverent outburst.

Brother Max abruptly stopped the sermon in mid-request.

Friends, Brother Max better *never* have to stop a sermon for a child's misbehavior.

Nevertheless, the sermon stopped in mid-sentence.

The temporary silence was deafening and Brother Max made a statement I remember till this day:

"I don't know whose child that is in our balcony, next to the air-conditioner," he intoned, *"but if the mother of that child would please remove him from our sanctuary, I would be glad to continue!"*

Needless to say, there were lots of mothers headed up those balcony stairs. Miss Norma Jane Eagerton, Miss Mary Dwozan, and Miss Martha Williams were among the unhappy group headed up those stairs, enroute to remedy this awful, embarrassing, humiliating situation, but it was *my* mother, Miss Martha" who won the prize that day!

Eat Here & Get Gas!

It was no surprise that Sunday afternoon was rough for me! All privileges were taken away for quite some time. It was years before I was permitted to sit anywhere in church other than at my mother's side.

I was quiet as the proverbial church mouse from that point forward. I couldn't sit in the same building with Russell.

When I finally gained enough of her confidence to again venture away from her (I was about 20), I cherished my earned freedom more than ever.

It didn't take too long until a new plan was conceived, this one outside the hallowed walls of the sancturary.

One day, I realized the church services were being broadcast over the local radio station. I came up with a plan to wait in the men's restroom until after services started; that kept me out of everyone's sight as they entered the church. Then, I slipped outside to my mother's car in the parking lot where the radio kept me updated on the progress of the sermon. Then, at the right moment, I dashed back into the men's room just ahead of the crowd leaving the sanctuary and simply mesh myself into the crowd exiting to the parking lot after church!

Not a bad plan for a little guy. Best part was it worked flawlessly for the remainder of my church childhood days. In fact, it worked so well that other friends began to follow my lead and we all joined up with the older guys who had driver's licenses and we all rode around during church time.

We even went down to Stuckey's and drank Cokes and fed the talking bird *(qwaaaakkkk)* ate free samples, and talked with the big guys; They included: Terry Coleman, later Representative Terry Coleman and Larry Jamieson, now Construction Company President Larry Jamieson among other lifelong friends from those days.

About a quarter before the hour, we'd start back toward the church. No real rush, Brother Max rarely finished before twelve, but, the radio broadcast stopped promptly at twelve and we couldn't be sure WHEN the service would actually end.

So, we'd hi-tail it back to the men's room at church a little before twelve, just in time to mingle with the exiting crowd again. It was ingenious! I was amazed that it worked as well as it did.

I thought Sunday mornings improved dramatically! My mother was never the wiser and I assume she must have thought I had learned my lesson to behave in church since she never heard me laugh out loud enough again to stop the service!

I haven't figured out an acceptable plan that will work successfully for adults as yet, but I am still looking.

Eat Here & Get Gas!

I do know that Drawing pictures of the Devil in the front cover of the Baptsit Hymnal isn't a good idea.

Fire for Effect!

Miss Sara was a treasure. People like her don't come along very often
CMW

Ghosts and goblins were everywhere around Eastman when I was growing up. Everywhere! Halloween was exciting. Fall festivals and people like Miss Nanny Daniels and Miss Sarah Bulloch and her family made it all the more interesting and exciting.

Miss Nanny was very creative. She was a dear friend of our family. Her husband, Marsden, was a very special man. He told me that when he was a boy, he had been on the train from Detroit to Chicago and actually shined both Henry Ford's and Thomas Edison's shoes. That made an everlasting impression on me. I had read about both these men in my history class just about that time and was impressed with Mr. Marsden from that point on! He was really high in my book. Always was!

And so was Miss Nanny. When it came time for a fall festival, I can remember her all dressed up in a gypsy costume, stirring a "witches' brew" kettle out at the National Guard Armory.

We didn't have any other building that many people could get into at one time, so the National

Charles M. Williams

Guard Armory was a community center of sorts in those days. All the military classrooms and offices were filled with gouls and goblins when Halloween came around. It was an amazing transformation.

Miss Nanny always had a distinctive, powerful voice and a serious Southern accent. She could make noises that would make a kid's skin crawl. And she did it year after year at the fall festival.

Little Jack's daddy would always participate, too. He was a great big man and had a very loud voice. He set up an old shrine ambulance, complete with a casket and a spook! Oh, man! It was great to grow up in a place like this, and the more I think about it, the more I realize how fortunate we all were. The adults were slightly touched, creative people, full of life and energy, and ready to have fun on a moment's notice. Certainly made life interesting for me and it probably explains a bit about the sense of humor I have enjoyed all these years.

The Bullochs were different. They were probably the first people I ever really recognized as "different" all by myself. There were lots of people about whom my friends would say, "Man, he's different But, the Bullochs, well you just kinda' knew down deep inside they were unusual people.

Miss Sara was a school teacher of the most wonderful kind. She taught everybody's mother and daddy and everybody loved and respected her. She was a tireless worker in the field of education, committed to the ideal that everyone should be able to read. In fact, adult literacy was among her most important contributions.

In a county where about 40 percent of the population doesn't have a high school diploma (even today), well, the fields were "ripe unto harvest" for Miss Sara. She never tired of her work, day in, day out, nights and weekends. The eccentric life she lived was just considered normal for her and her family.

Her husband was the original Quixotic character. For about as far back as I can remember, he was seen most every day, his tall, thin frame, walking up and down the streets with his head bowed, rarely ever stopping to talk and almost never raising his chin from his chest.

His frayed, old, dark three piece suit flapped with the breeze of his motion, and he looked the part of the ancient mariner always in search of someone to engage in conversation. If one ever was so engaged, there would be talk of investment banking and overseas trade and an infamous banking house in Atlanta with geo-thermal interests. 'Heady stuff for a kid in Eastman to hear about from this elderly gentleman.

The Bullochs lived in what is known as the "Old Eastman House" on Eastman Way. That house was built in the 1800s and was, just on that account, a spooky place.

Today, it serves as the local historical *(some folk's refer to it as the Hysterical)* society's base of operations.

The building stands two stories high and to a small child, it was imposing and in need of a coat of paint and a crew of vine rippers on duty for a month. It was, to say the least, the last place anyone wanted to go on Halloween.

In fact, it seemed it *always* was Halloween at that house in the swirling imagination of an impressionable young boy.

One year, Miss Bulloch turned loose her sons, Carey *(the son most like his father, black suit and all, and younger son Robert, not like anyone else I have yet encountered),* to create a genuine house of horrors for Halloween.

Understand, these were young men of above-average intelligence and enormous creativity nurtured by a similarly-creative and loving mother!

Trust me. It didn't take much of an imagination to turn this house into the ultimate Halloween horror. The house was already dark and there were plenty of things to trip over including an ancient white Buick covered with grass and vines.

Carey and Robert added dozens of finishing touches to their "house of horrors" with capes and curtains and ketchup and magic and rattling bones and gory sound effects.

'Made quite an impression on me. I never remember being more filled with fear in my life.

Eat Here & Get Gas!

The combination of light and darkness, the strange interior of that house, the recorded sound effects, the curtains, the lanterns, it was more than I had ever encountered before on any Halloween experience. Those boys had put together a benchmark for Halloween evenings in Eastman. It was terrifying. It became an icon!

The following Saturday matinee was another Vincent Price thriller, and I thought, somebody ought to take this guy to the Bulloch's. These folks had a natural edge on this kind of thing. I figured they could teach ole' Vince a thing or two he could use!

More than 40 years have passed, so have Mr. and Mrs. Bulloch. Both boys have grown up and left, Robert is a museum curator, quite a natural choice. Carey, no doubt is an international merchant banker with a dark three piece suit, and geo-thermal interests, yet, I remember that house and that night, vividly. It was a step into creativity that I had not previously encountered. I was both scared and mesmerized.

As teen-agers, Halloween took on a different slant for the boys I hung around with. Fall festivals were not nearly as much fun, probably because sophisticated young minds like ours could usually recognize monsters in masks and bloody costumes.

Most of the time bobbing for apples resulted in the need for CPR so other avenues had to be explored for teenagers.

Water balloons and firecrackers, toilet paper rollings, and something like gang competitions started up in fun, but it could get pretty serious.

One night, Little Jack, David, Sonny, Dickie Richard, the McDaniel Brothers and dozens of other high-school aged boys and I gathered up for the ultimate Halloween event.

It all started with water balloons and firecrackers. Of course Little Jack had an arsenal that escalated to simple mortars made from those '50s-version aluminum drinking cups, a wooden crochet ball and M-80 firecrackers that were extremely powerful.

Sam McDaniel showed us that by burying the cup in the dirt up to it's rim, dropping in a lit M-80, slamming a wooden crochet ball (just about the perfect size of the drinking cup), and slamming it into the cup with an entrenching tool (army surplus the McDaniel brothers conveniently had handy).

When the explosion occurred, the wooden crochet ball actually disappeared into the sky.

We quickly learned that by angling the cup, the ball followed a simple trajectory that would generally land it in a targeted area. It was in fact a precursor to the Viet Nam era Mortar Round! The anticipation was a rival camp, certainly not

Eat Here & Get Gas!

anyone's home, especially while local widow women gathered for coffee.

No concern was ever given for the impact such a heavy wooden object falling from several hundred feet could impart, let alone the dangers or damage that could result to one's head should providence allow such connections, *naaaaaah!*

Angle the cup, drop in the lit M-80, drop in the ball, slam it down with the intrenching tool, step back, and watch it disappear.

We were fortunate. No one was ever killed or injured by this prank. However, the roof damage was significant and the beautiful, expensive, glass topped table was destroyed. The sight of half a dozen ladies in evening attire jumping through open windows was a sight to behold.

No one ever found out who had fired the crochet ball. No one was injured. And, nobody ever mentioned it again. Better judgement took over after that, and the idea of McDaniel M-80 mortars was forgotten.

The lesson I got from all these experiences was that you can have fun, you can be creative, you can enjoy yourself without hurting other people or property. In fact, there might even be ways to harness all that creativity and enjoyment in the art of helping other people.

Miss Sara was a master in that art. Maybe there is hope for people like me, and you, geothermally speaking, of course.

Just a simple, screened porch

The first time you will know exactly what it costs to complete a construction project is about one year after you finish
CMW

There is always more than one way to look at anything, and then there is the way my wife wants to look at things. Of course, the *"thing"* can be absolutely *anything*.

For example, we've added to our home recently. We started building our home 20 years ago and waited all these years to finish the project. We thought we would pay off the original debt and have enough set aside to pay for the new construction.

That's as good an excuse as I can come up with at the moment. So, after all this time, we are underway. Things like "mudding the sheetrock" and installing septic systems, and all the many fun projects associated with additions and renovations. Tear out perfectly good "stuff" 'cause it isn't what or where something just has to be in accordance with the new plan. It's like a stock broker arrangement: doesn't matter if they are putting together or taking apart, the cost meters are still running at high speed!

At the outset, all *I ever* really wanted to add was a great big, wonderful, screened-in porch. Just a place for rocking chairs, ceiling fans, all there, positioned to provide an incredible view of our beautiful pond.

That pond is 37 acres, and our two sons have grown up water skiing out there with their friends. Just a porch, nothing exceptional. I always imagined it would be located next to the kitchen where cool drinks could always be handy and easy to get to!

Nothing fancy, just a porch. Certainly, to get a porch like I envisioned, I was agreeable to also add a bedroom.

Of course. Just a nice, simple, big room called a master bedroom. Sure, that would be great. And while we're at it, we could add another bathroom.

Oh, why not. That would really be nice, put a little shower in there, another commode. Ah, yes! Great idea. And why not another clothes closet? Everyone needs closet space. A *big* closet would be even better. Huge and humongous are small words compared to the eventual size of this closet. A family of four could live in this closet. Twelve if they were Mexican.

"Still more closets," Charlotte suggested. Yes. Of course dear. A closet near the exterior door would be handy for coats and boots and things. A new spot for the washer and dryer. (The old spot for those machines was originally planned as a

Eat Here & Get Gas!

service hall and we *really need* that to service a dining room we don't have...or need!)

Why not another closet for "stuff" and a new hot water heater to supply the water for the new *whirlpool bath*. 'Not just a tub, mind you, but a gigantic, indoor *hot-tub* with swirling water and additional heating capacity to keep the water hot after its already been heated with your new water heater. Remember the new, huge, water heater?

And why not a steam generator to fill the shower cubicle, like Noah measured cubits, you know. Let's make it huge, with steam. Who knows why, but let's get one, because it would be much more expensive to add one later. Do it now while you can do it for only *this* extravagant amount. An installation later would be an even more outrageously extravagant amount!

And insulation. Let's just fill the walls with insulation and make it incredibly thick, tight, sound proof, cool in the summer, warm in the winter. Expensive now? Oh yes, but all the way to cost prohibitive later!

And, since we are going to have to build a roof out to connect to the garage because we can't walk in the rain to the car, you know, why not expand that roof just a bit while we're at it and say, build that dining area that we don't need, don't have furniture for, and will likely never use. You know the drill by now, "won't add much to the cost at this point but it sure would be expensive later on.

We can easily install air conditioning ducts to the new dining room and have them built into the slab while we're at it. Won't add much to the cost at this point; Be ridiculously expensive later. Get the expansion picture?

You know, that roof on the garage will have to be replaced pretty soon anyway, so, let's just go ahead, rip it off, and build a new roof over it. That won't add much while we're at it and it will of course, cost lots more later. Plus, the roof line can be made the same and it will all look much better. 'Always cheaper to do it now, you know.

'Better to separate the air conditioning from the old house. It will be more comfortable, more easily controlled, and it won't cost much more at this point, but it will be *virtually impossible later,* not to mention much more expensive if we were to wait, naturally.

All I really wanted was a porch, remember? Just a simple, wonderful, screened-in room with grand old rocking chairs and, did I mention a fireplace on the porch with expensive French doors that open out and a new, bigger, much bigger patio.

And, and, and...It is sometimes difficult to remember this project started out as a porch. But, and a very important **BUT** thought it is, Miss Charlotte is really happy, except now we have to

Eat Here & Get Gas!

have ceramic tile installed on the porch, along with outdoor porch wicker and rattan furniture, Hunter fans, straight backed rocking chairs (thank goodness my sister sent those as a delightful house warming gift), and decorations, curtains, and blinds…

And now we need those *(You fill in the blanks here)* and the *(Keep that imagination going)* And, there are the *(how's your imagination holding here…I bet better than my construction account).*

But of course, we must have *(Keep that imagination working…Charlotte has).* Isn't renovation and construction just what you'd like to start?

Just remember, even though it's ridiculously expensive now, it'll cost enormously more if you wait to finish this part before you start!

It's a fact many American's have learned the hard way.

Want to learn more? Just start a home renovation project.

You can *build* on it!

Skelton Ears

There is a powerful spirit that is the thread of generations
Martha Skelton Williams

It sits out in front of my home now, silently watching people come and go, greeting each one as they arrive and wishing traveling mercies on those who leave with a fond wish for friends to come back soon and often.

Only occasionally does it arouse the interest of some inquisitive youngster who cannot resist the temptation to hear her sound…

That old bell sits in a bricked casing, patiently waiting for whatever comes, but it wasn't always that way.

In 1905, that old bell was forged by Meneely & Company, Troy, N.Y. Who its original owners were, why they had it created and for what purpose, I may never know, any more than I might learn about the subsequent owners and their stories. The important point is that it came to be a part of our family one night in a camp house sitting atop one of the steep turns the Ocmulgee River makes as a part of Dodge County's southwestern border with neighboring Wilcox.

The regular weekly poker game was at its height. Ancient Age and Old Charter were pouring freely. Rumor has it that my dad, a regular player, was among the high rollers that night, as was the owner of the camp house.

Hand after hand was played and the pot grew to several thousands of dollars, which, was a very significant amount of money at the time. Eventually, the pot grew to a point where the owner of the house, feeling pretty good about his hand, I suppose, or making a powerful stand at bluffing the other players, "put up" and included the camp house to cover his bet.

I can't verify the story, but as legend has it, the bluff didn't stand. My dad's hand was better or he was a better poker bluffer and he won the pot, which included the camp house and this rather remarkable old bell perched at the top of an old, wooden tower.

This is a story about that old bell!

Over the next several years, the camp house became a regular recreational spot for our family and my dad's business friends. I was a boy of maybe 13 or so along about then. Those were days of wonder! That camp house, which had so mysteriously come to belong to my folks, was a place of genuine excitement, relaxation, adventure and endless curiosity.

My folks went there several times each week to cook a steak and party with friends.

I went along and took one or two of my friends, and as the partying took over the better judgment of the adults, my friends and I took over the cars or

Eat Here & Get Gas!

boats or farm animals and explored all the possibilities we either found or created.

One of our very favorite things to do was to climb up the old 30-foot wooden tower to ring that huge old bell at the top. 'Probably weighed 600 pounds, and we often wondered how and why they got it up that high in the first place.

Fact is, that old bell could be rung from its high tower and heard for miles up and down that river. No doubt, it was some kind of signal from years gone by.

Imagination can take off from this point. I can recall visions of murder mysteries and romance novels and clandestine spy meetings, all centered around that old bell.

Drinking and driving don't mix. I have often wondered how it was that no automobile accidents occurred during those many trips home from the riverhouse. Often, the drivers were practically inebriated and operating new, fast, big-engine high-powered cars.

There were many treacherous curves in the road home, but by the grace of the good Lord, it never happened. Nothing else could explain it!

My dad decided to sell the river house in the late1960s. By then, it had more than served its purpose: the parties, the poker games, the fishing trips, and other things that really shouldn't be mentioned.

After all, he owned the old house for several years and he probably decided he could use the money better elsewhere, likely in his dream to own his retirement home at Daytona Beach, Florida.

Not to mention that someone must have offered him a ridiculous profit on the property. He let my mother know his intentions and to my surprise, she didn't disagree. All she wanted from the property was that old bell perched up on that rickety old wooden tower.

"The property has been sold as it is, *bell included!* Leave the (&%$#) bell alone," were his words, but friends, those words fell on "Skelton" ears. (Skelton was my mother's maiden name and in our family, it meant being stubborn, determined, focused, will not be denied, and all the other words you can use to say *"don't bet on it!"*

That Skelton blood simmered a bit biding its time, and in a few weeks, when my dad was out of town for the day, my mother took two men from the Ford place along with the company's old wrecker, and headed for the river-house.

It was just a few days ahead of the pending sale. My mother was quite discouraged to discover the wrecker boom was not nearly tall enough to reach above the bell to lift it off its perch on top of the tower. How in the world would she get the powerful lifting force of the wrecker up above the bell so it could be lifted up and carried it home?

There were two choices: Choice "A" would be to lift the wrecker up above the bell. Choice "B" would be to get the bell below the wrecker.

Choice "B" was the chosen solution and the old wrecker was used to physically pull the bell down, tower and all, totally destroying the tower and rendering virtually useless the solid steel brackets that supported the bell in the first place. (It all came crashing down with a resounding, reverberating sound that was, no doubt, heard up and down the river as it echoed around the bends and curves for miles!

'No matter. The object of the "Skelton" exercise was to take that bell home. Period.

With hard work, a straining wrecker, ingenuity, and a personality that simply would not be denied, it happened.

After broken parts were loaded onto the back of the vehicle, the bell itself hoisted behind the wrecker, and the strong and stately old tower that had withstood decades of weather and abuse all in shambles lying about the ground, the little procession was headed away from it's stately home for no telling how many decades. That bell was headed for its new home, the *Skelton* way!

Needless to say, my dad was not pleased.

But no matter, that old bell became a part of the family where it has remained for the past four decades.

Charles M. Williams

In my lifetime, it will sit and greet visitors, wishing them well as they come and leave, and always serving as a gentle reminder of the powerful, stubborn, and fiercely-determined spirits that dwell here.

"Wish I hadn't done that"

The only people who don't make mistakes are the ones who don't do nothin! The trick is to learn from 'em. Don't repeat 'em and straighten' 'em out when you can.
Vernon Williams

Mr. Norman was the most energetic man I ever met. He farmed. He drove a red and white Ford pick-up truck and drove it fast. He had to. He had fields to tend, miles to cover, and IRS agents to avoid.

To see him pass by at less-than-break-neck speed was a pretty good indication that he was either very ill or his truck wasn't running right. And, if it wasn't running right, he immediately traded it in for one exactly like the last one, unless there was a bigger engine available.

In very short order, he had it three inches thick with dust so that no one could tell the difference between old and new. Then he'd run a little faster to make up for lost time.

Mr. Norman was a hustler. He had to be. With four sons and one daughter, and more land to tend than anyone I ever knew, he was the farmer of his times. He was good at it. He was prosperous and profitable. He always had sun-burnt skin peeling off his nose and under his eyes. He had a smile and something funny to say every time I ever saw him, except once.

Aside from his large farming operation Mr. Norman also rented additional acreage from other people, people like my dad who owned land but didn't farm it.

Often, after the corn was gathered, Mr. Norman turned hogs on the field to let them fatten up. When he did that, he would bring a feeder and set it up on the property. Nothing unusual here, just a kind of tank with doors that the hogs knew instinctively how to open to get to the food and supplements.

I don't know why or how it happened, but an older friend and I were riding through the fields on a little motorcycle with a .22 rifle in search of targets.

Fortunately, we didn't see a hog but we did stumble on that shiny metal hog feeder and the temptation was just too great.

Boxes of shells later, that's about 250 shots, that shiny new feeder was riddled with bullet holes. Although the feeder was not more than 20 yards from us, (we could've just as easily hit it with a rock), it was seen as a real challenge to shoot up and destroy and for whatever reason, we did so with a vengeance.

Proud of ourselves and out of shells, we overloaded the little motorcycle again and went bouncing away over the terraces and on to other

Eat Here & Get Gas!

adventures never giving a second thought to the property we had wantonly destroyed.

Within a few days, Mr. Norman, ever on his path to check on things in and around his operations, discovered the destruction and mentioned it to my dad who quickly figured out pretty much what had taken place.

He brought me to task in front of Mr. Norman. I did the only thing I knew to do. I lied and lied and lied and said I didn't know anything about it and that I would sure be on the lookout for anybody who might be responsible for such an irresponsible act. As you already know, Eddie Haskell from the Leave it to Beaver TV program, had indeed made an impression on me by then. "Why no Missus Cleaver *(Mr. Hardy)* I can't imagine.

I knew then and I know now that both my dad and Mr. Norman probably knew *pretty well* what happened.

What I didn't know was that they knew *in fact*.

I "got away with it" at the time, but not really!

You see, it's still on my slate after four decades, and both the men have been dead and gone for most of that time... and that's the point:

I not only didn't "get away with anything," but I *still* have an old scar there to remind me that I didn't. I have known for a long time it would have been far better to have cleared it up when I had the chance.

Charles M. Williams

All of us make mistakes. The defining moments of our lives are what we do *when* we make mistakes. Do we hide them? Do we deny them? Do we own up to them, suffer the consequences, and grow as a result of them?

It's a question posed to every person. The answers are very important. A good night's sleep with a clear conscious is more valuable than money in the bank. It lasts longer than a well earned thrashing!

It is a lesson learned late and carried long.

Field of Fire

It was NOT cigarettes...at least on this particular occasion
Albert Glass, Jr.

It was windy that day. Everybody thought we were smoking cigarettes and of course, we were. They also thought that *that* was what caused the incident, but it wasn't.

Little Albert and I had been longtime friends. Our dads were drinking buddies and we had tried our luck with hot beer (we found we could grab a can or two, toss them out the bedroom window of the camp house while the parents were in another room partying). Cigarettes were easy then, just swipe a pack or two of Parliaments from his mothers pocketbook and a pack of Camels from my dad's cigarette drawer. It was simple to get cigarettes and "very cool" to smoke them. Sort of lost the "challenge" though, when we discovered beer. Besides, we were beginning to notice girls and to think and talk and dream about them.

On this particular March day, we discovered this abandoned water tank lying in the middle of a pasture near my parent's home. The old tank was about 30 feet long and maybe eight feet in diameter. You could tell it was on its side because there was a square opening which was almost at ground level.

Little Albert and I saw this tank as the absolutely perfect fort! Oh the power of imagination! We thought we could take on the world from that fortress. We could blow German U-Boats out of the North Atlantic, repel Apache Indian attacks from our Fort Laramie, effectively bomb Japanese targets from our B-29 flying fortress, and readily fly missions into outer space from our Mercury rocket spacecraft.

If that wasn't enough, we thought we could penetrate Russian harbors with our nuclear submarine. What an opportunity we found lying on its side.

Of course, we would be able to smoke cigarettes and cigars inside without fear of observation. (We never once thought about the smoke pouring out of that opening or the fact that we would be inundated by the smoke-filled cylinder). We focused more on talk about the alluring qualities of the women, actually 13-year-old girls, we desired most.

But first things first. We had to prepare the vehicle. Hours were invested in crude tools such as ax handles and bricks, to create leverage to return our vehicle to its proper, upright position.

Great creativity was summoned for two relatively light-weight young boys to actually accomplish anything with this massive object, yet, as the hours passed and morning changed to early and mid-afternoon, we not only turned the great machine to its majestic and upright condition, we had enough foresight to chock the huge cylinder to help it remain in place.

'What a wonderful sight. Our goal was established *and* accomplished. It is a great feeling to create a plan and see it to its end. The memory of the hard work dissipated quickly in light of our achievement.

Only one daunting task remained: We had to create a cover to shield from the elements and inquisitive eyes that might enter the square hole at the top of this great vehicle of childhood imagination!

Without a drill or screws or hinges or materials from which to form a satisfactory door, we scavenged nearby barns and old buildings for a suitable cover, finding only a piece of soft spongy rubber. We quickly decided this would solve all our problems. By setting the rubber on fire, we decided the hot part would become very sticky and could thus attach itself to the outside steel shell of the great machine.

We really believed it would work, but we couldn't get our matches to ignite beside the "vehicle." There was too much wind that day and it kept blowing out our matches before the rubber material would ignite.

So, we decided to carry the spongy rubber material across the field, get behind a an old abandoned tobacco barn shelter about a hundred yards away. There we figured we could shield the rubber mat from the wind in order to burn the edge of the "door" and make it liquid, and we figured, sticky!

Great idea! That part worked perfectly. The rubber material began to burn a little bit and we were excited. We took off across the dry grass for the great machine to attach our wonderful cover.

Naturally, as we dashed across the very dry grass in the gusting wind, the fire began to consume the rubber and it dripped a firey rubber trail behind us for about 100 yards. We didn't notice the fire that was following us until we got almost all the way back to the "vehicle."

Little Albert took off his shirt and began to beat the flames while I continued on to the great machine with the burning rubber. I could see no use in wasting the opportunity for sticking the cover in its rightful place. No matter that I was spreading liquid fire in dry grass on a very windy day.

Fact is, the rubber did stick to the great machine, but only until it had cooled again. Unfortunately, I could hardly see the result of our great accomplishment, for the smoke and flames and rapidly spreading wildfire that now raged across the 50-acre field headed for nearby homes and forest lands.

The event also excited the forestry department. Local volunteer firefighters, Forestry doziers-

Eat Here & Get Gas!

operators, and all those curious people who were immediately attracted to the billowing smoke seemed to come out of nowhere.

My dad was excited too when he learned there were no injuries and no significant property damage.

However, he was in no mood to buy a story about a doorway for the great vehicle as he unbuckled his belt…

Brother Dave

*I just don't want to get to the end of the game
and wonder what might have been
if only I had made myself try!*
CMW

I think I was in elementary school when I first realized how much I enjoyed being up in front of audiences. Fifth grade. Joyce Jones was my teacher, and she was excellent.

I realized how much fun it was for me to do things that made people laugh. More often than not, my antics aroused the ire of my teachers and resulted in some form of punishment, and notwithstanding the eventual problems low conduct grades inevitably produced at home.

Still, I kept at it. I had the privilege of seeing Brother Dave Gardner live and in person in Daytona Beach...Seabreeze Auditorium...in the early 1960's! Our family loved Daytona. My dad owned several houses there and throughout his life wanted to retire there.

In the early 1960's, we spent every summer at the beach and it was on one of these occasions that I was privileged to actually see and hear Brother Dave.

My sister Pat knew I had listened to all the Brother Dave albums. She had managed to get tickets to his live program and made arrangements with our parents to let her take me to see him. Without question, it changed my life forever!

Then I "grew up" and along came work and the complications of family and business and recreation and first thing you know, the idea of picking and singing and all that simply didn't stay near the "front burner."

Turns out, a friend of mine, Bill Torrance, was getting ready to entertain at an Old Time Barnyard Festival, "Mossy Creek", in October 1987. He and I sat down and played and sang together a little bit and he invited me to get on stage with him to play and sing for a real, live audience.

Even though I hadn't done it since elementary school days and I was scared to death, I jumped at the chance! It was thrilling to have people actually listening to me and applauding my meager efforts, laugh at stories and enjoy my songs. I was hooked immediately. Just simply couldn't wait for the next opportunity.

I listened to every speaker I could find either on tape, TV, in person, or in movies and I tried to learn what I could from their material, their deliveries, and their organization. I studied everything I could find to adopt, steal, modify, and learn to make my "stuff" work! I listened to every speaker, entertainer, humorist and singer I could.

One of my favorites was a man from "Arabi" Georgia, the "Minister of Myrth", an ordained

Eat Here & Get Gas!

Baptist Minister, Wayne Aytes. I heard Wayne speaking to a group at Middle Georgia College one night in the late '80s and got almost as excited as when I had heard Brother Dave back in my early teens. Wayne has this enormous depth and understanding of the mind of an inebriated person, and his voice has that distinctive, "I've been there" quality, that makes his portrayal of a funny drunk come to life.

I wanted to emulate that characteristic. I have tried for years with some success and I have never missed with that style of humor. Wayne is still very active in the speaking and entertainment circuits across the country. He is one of my very favorites!

Carl Hurley has the most delightful delivery of anyone I have ever heard. His enthusiasm for the stories he tells and his sheer enjoyment of telling them is readily apparent the entire time he speaks. He enjoys them so much that **he** laughs in the delivery. I think that is special and find myself unable to do otherwise. 'Seems to me that if someone is thoroughly enjoying something, everyone watching and listening can't help but do the same thing!

The great "Red" Skelton (no relation unfortunately), regularly laughed at himself during his stage acts. What an entertainer! He has long been a model for the idea of "Good, Clean Fun!"

Charles M. Williams

There is an undertaker from Alabama whom I had the chance to hear at a Chamber banquet several years ago. He did something I thought was absolutely outstanding. He did his entire program using a *wireless*, hand-held microphone, no notes of any kind, and he didn't remain at a podium. In fact, he walked all around the room. I was impressed. I wondered if I could ever do that! I just had to try, but with a guitar?

Brooks Coleman is a state representative from Duluth, Georgia. Brooks is the most enthusiastic, excited, motivated individual I have had the pleasure to witness first-hand. His enthusiasm is contagious. He is very excited, so how can anyone near him be anything but excited? And his messages about his hero, "Roy Rogers" are outstanding thoughts for audiences everywhere.

One other speaker I have heard and tried to emulate is the former coach of the Notre Dame Football team, the 155-pound fireball, Lou Holtz. What an incredible positive message. What a powerful delivery. What an incredibly positive human being. What an awesome impression he makes on audiences.

The insanity of Ray Stevens with his novelty songs like Ahab the Arab, the Mississippi Squirrel, and of course, my very favorite, *It's me again, Mawgritt*, are all crowd-pleasers and I have worked hard to do justice to those tunes.

Eat Here & Get Gas!

I love the mellow vocals of John Denver, the guitar mastery of Chet Atkins, the simplicity of Merle Travis as both a picker and a songwriter; songs like "16 Tons".

There is just so much music and so many musical styles you can learn to appreciate.

Hank Williams' simple chords and his clear, concise writing style are all-time favorites of mine. That beautiful, haunting voice of the one and only Patsy Cline is unsurpassed, and Merle Haggard is the all time leader in "live the life you write about" classical country music.

Gosh, there is only so much time in any given program, you know!

If I had to pick an absolute favorite, it would have to be from my teenage days. There were the Beach Boys, Chuck Berry, Elvis Presley, the Dave Clarke Five, the Animals, The Rolling Stones., but nothing made such an impression on me as the Beatles.

Now, what all that has to do with "stand up" is more than I can explain, but any show I have the privilege to do has at least some if not all those ingredients stirred together with my own "Down Home" imagination.

So far so good. After more than 20 years, I am still looking forward to becoming an overnight success. 'Fact is, the success I have enjoyed to-date is more than enough and whatever follows will be enjoyed to the fullest.

Charles M. Williams

The joy of the journey is not the getting there *but the traveling!* I plan to keep travelling every single day of my life and I hope you will as well.

Do you choose to lift or lean?

Life is a series of choices. Once made, the consequences are yours forever.
CMW

Charlotte, (my little girlfriend from about age nine) and I got married in 1970. She was (and still is) a month or so older than me. Let me tell you, we were all smiles about the future and so filled with love and enthusiasm we could see only the positive sides of everything!

What an exciting time.

Why is it that too many of us allow that enthusiasm and excitement for each other to slip away? Could it be that our spouses get older and seem to become less physically attractive? I ain't sure about you, but I sure have noticed that I don't seem to be as firm in most of my body parts as I was 25 or more years ago myself!

'Fact is, I probably wasn't as physically perfect in reality as my memory tells me anyway.

The point is, that's a pretty weak argument for allowing enthusiasm and commitment in a relationship to slip away! I don't believe we stop laughing because we get old! I believe we get old because we stop laughing! The same is true for enthusiasm in our relationships.

Could it be that many traditional married couples simply take each other so much for granted and for whatever reason, decide to stop "dating" each other after they are married?

Can't you remember how exciting it was to go out on a date together, just to be near that very special person and to smell their special perfume or aftershave?

Don't you remember how you could hardly wait for the next time to be together? It made little difference what the two of you were doing together, it was just being near that special person. Remember? Where does all that excitement and enthusiasm go? Better question is *why* do we let it leave?

I can imagine you're thinking it goes to mortgage payments and laundry and cooking and working and lawns and bills and medical expenses and car payments and school and babies and pages and pages of thing after thing to a list that could go on for miles.

The sad thing is, letting it go was a choice. Conscious or not, intentional or not, like it or not, it is a choice each partner makes, every day, all year long, year after year.

Then, one day, as a result of all those little choices, that person who so thrilled you and enticed you and appealed to you is no longer your choice!

We are all the results of our choices and recognizing that, *today, I choose to be enthusiastic* about my relationship with my wife of more than 30 years.

I choose to be positive.

I choose to be enthusiastic.

I choose to love my wife.

I choose to date my wife and treat her like a queen.

It is a choice, a conscious, deliberate choice that I made today. I can't tell you what the situation will be tomorrow, but for today, I choose to be enthusiastic about our relationship and I plan to treat her like a queen. If tomorrow comes for me, I hope I will wake up with exactly the same idea, but tomorrow is only a promise. Today is all I can deal with.

I have made that choice *every* day for more than 30 years of marriage.

My sons must make their own choices *but* they have a picture presented every day of a father who is in love with and very enthusiastic about their mother. I cannot make their choices, but I can make mine and I choose to be enthusiastic and very excited about life in general and Charlotte in particular. *It is a choice!*

I am constantly amazed when people ask me, "what (drug) are you taking?" Thinking I must be on some "upper" to be as enthusiastic about things as I am. "Whatever it is, I want to bottle it and take it and sell it to other people…"

What a compliment! What a powerful statement, but the fact is, the only drug is *choice*.

As Abraham Lincoln said, *"Most people are about as happy as they want to be!"* I disagree to an extent. You see, I want to be much happier than I think I am, and I'm working on it!

We have a right, based on our Constitution, not to *be* happy, but to *pursue* happiness. I like to think of myself in Ray Stevens' zaney line from Ahab the Arab, as being in *"hot pursuit!"* (*"With the Sultan's whole army in hot pursuit…on and on they ran)*

There is a well known example of two brothers, one extremely positive and the other, highly pessimistic. One Christmas, the boy's parents decided to see how the distinctly-opposite personalities would react if the pessimistic child got every toy he ever wanted all wrapped in beautiful paper waiting for him on Christmas morning while the very optimistic child, received something as negative as shoe boxes full of horse manure.

On Christmas morning, as the pessimistic child looked at all the beautiful boxes and found all his fabulous toys, he began to complain about them being wrapped wrong and that they probably would not last or they were the wrong ones or they were too whatever…and on and on and on!

Eat Here & Get Gas!

The positive child found the one shoe box full of horse manure and immediately ran out of the house to the barn, and was found searching through every stall and pen.

His dad stopped him and asked, "Son, what *are* you looking for?"

The very positive little guy said, "Dad, with this much horse manure, I know there's got to be a pony here somewhere!"

That is what making a choice is all about. That little guy made a conscious choice. He chose to be positive and enthusiastic and found something to be excited about!

What is your choice every day? If life hands you a box of horse manure, and of course it can and does on occasion, do you gripe and complain, or do you dash out in search of that proverbial pony that just *has* to be there somewhere?

It is a choice. *Your* choice.

Choosing to be positive is an *attitude*. It is a way of life that you are free to choose this day, right now.

Choosing to be enthusiastic is an attitude. And of course, *attitude is everything*.

There is a great poem I chanced upon from a little collection my mother kept in her night stand drawer throughout her life. The poem title asks the question: "Which are you?" by Ella Wheeler Wilcox. Ask yourself that question as you read her words:

Charles M. Williams

There are two kinds of people on earth today.
Just two kinds of people, no more I say.

Not the sinner and saint, for it's well understood,
The good are half bad, and the bad are half good.

Not the rich and the poor, for to rate a man's wealth,
You must first know the state of his conscience and health.

Not the humble and proud, for in life's little span,
Who puts on vain airs, is not counted a man.
Not the happy and sad, for the swift flying years
Bring each man his laughter and each man his tears.

No, the two kinds of people on earth I mean,
Are the people who lift and the people who lean.

Wherever you go, you will find the earth's masses are always divided in just these two classes.

And, oddly enough, you will find, too, I've seen,
There's only one lifter to twenty who lean.

Eat Here & Get Gas!

In which class are you? Are you easing the load
Of overtaxed lifters, who toil down the road?

Or are you a leaner, who lets others share your portion of labor and worry and care?

It really is a matter of attitude. It's a matter of choice.
Today *I choose* to be a lifter.
I choose to have a positive attitude.
Today *I choose* to pursue happiness.
Today *I choose* to share a kind word with others.
Today *I choose* to be enthusiastic.
Today *I choose* to kindle that excitement with my wife of 30 years.
Today *I choose* to encourage you to make these same choices.

It will affect your attitude. It can most assuredly change your life for the better! What is even more amazing is the effect it can have on all those people you come into contact, but it must and in fact can only start with you.

Baby Elephants know

"The saddest part is the simple fact that it doesn't have to be that way"
CMW

One of the saddest stories I have ever read is about baby elephants. Elephants are creatures that have survived since long before the earliest recorded times. Their ancient ancestors can be found in the most primitive history books, those pictures drawn on the walls by caveman.

Huge, powerful, massive, beautiful animals, elephants are to me among the most pitied creatures on Earth.

You see, when a very young elephant is to be trained for a circus, it is tied to a huge, heavy stake driven deep into the ground. This stake can easily hold fast against a far larger animal than the young, small elephant. The actual fastening is accomplished with a rope or cable which is impossible for the animal to break.

Tug, pull, fight, bite, dig, squall, and whatever else the small elephant may try, the oversized stake and the massive tie are absolutely impossible for it to budge.

Squat, strain, rip, and tear for as long as it may dare, there is no give in the stake, regardless of the effort put forth by the animal.

Charles M. Williams

As time passes, the animal comes to regard the harness and the stake as the absolutely impossible obstacles that they are. The elephant eventually accepts its new reality. For all practical purposes, the elephant simply resigns itself to the fact that the stake is immovable and the tie is unbreakable, so any further effort on his or her part is utterly futile.

It is at this point the game is over.

For you see, as the animal grows with this mindset of total defeat, the trainers can then replace the massive stake and the huge, heavy tie with smaller, and less-substantial equipment.

And, even as the elephant grows and becomes ever stronger, it still regards the stake and tie as an utterly impossible obstacle, without regard to their decreasing size and strength.

The end result is that a massive, fully-grown, incredibly-powerful elephant can be held fast even by a tiny stake and a small rope.

Think about that fact for a moment!

Don't you see?

It's always too soon to quit!

What does all this mean?

It is a very simple but accurate illustration of the enormous power self-perception. And guess what, it doesn't apply exclusively to elephants!

What a sad story; to think that through years and years of negative feedback and training, this absolutely magnificent and powerful creature one of the strongest if not the strongest animal on Earth, is trained to believe he is defeated and thus allow such weak shackles to hold him fast.

How much sadder it is that even more powerful creatures called humans, are held by even weaker shackles called thoughts and attitudes.

Tell a child that he or she is worthless and you drive a stake in the ground that a full grown bull elephant *can not* remove. Reinforce that rope with other negative comments about that child and you'll weave a chain that a fast moving freight train could not break.

Continue such shameful treatment of this child and you will soon see a young adult with shackles too weak to be true but too strong to be broken.

You will see this young person, at the very least, limiting himself or herself and, at worst, harming themselves or others.

I am not a psychologist, but I understand how important self esteem is. I have seen the devastating effects of low self-esteem. I have seen, first hand, the result of negative messages.

The saddest part is the simple fact that it doesn't have to be this way. Statues and history books are for the politicians and heros.

My goal has never been to hold power over others or to have people come to me for judgments.

Quite the contrary, I simply advocate the concept of making the world a little better starting here and now *with me.*

To that end I make simple commitments every day:

I will, this day, commit myself to positive thoughts.

I will, this day, have something good to say to everyone with whom I come into contact.

I will, this day, be an encourager and not a discourager, a lifter, not a leaner.

Today, I will read!

I will listen to but will not simply accept what the media or other people say.

I will read! I believe it's time we all realized that the only difference between the person you are today and the person you will be five years in the future is based on the people you meet and the books you read! READ.

Just as Miss Sarah Bulloch realized all those years ago, reading is the foundation for knowledge and understanding. What a genuine individual she was; an educator, a teacher, a friend, a person who took all that she was given and recycled it to those who needed it more.

If there were more Sarah Bullochs in the world, there would be less poverty, less misery, and more love for our fellow men. She spent the years most people sit down, by standing up and teaching others to read! What a lady. What an inspiration!

Eat Here & Get Gas!

I mention Miss Sara again here to provide an excellent example of one person who made choices daily. She could've propped her feet up. Instead, she got busy looking for people whom she could help.

Shackles and ropes were her forte. Removing the ties that bind people to illiteracy was her cause. Helping people become better than they were was her life's work.

Here's a question for you: "What stakes are holding you tightly to the ground?" What ropes of attitude and low self-esteem are holding you back? What are you going to do about them? Remember, positive thinking weakens false shackles. Don't give in to your limitations.

More than likely, and I'd be willing to bet, they only exist in your mind!

This ever-changing world

'The more things change, the more they remain the same.
CMW

It's funny the things we remember. Of course, I should have received more whippings than I did for the mischief I caused, but it works out somehow!

I guess it has helped me to be somewhat more understanding of my sons through the experiences of their childhood, teen-age and young adult years.

When Chip was born in May 1977, I was about as unprepared to be a father as any man could be. That old saying, "anyone can be a daddy. But, being a father, that's different," was a sign of things to come for me!

When Dr. Oscar Spivey handed me that little red-faced bundle of wrinkles for the first time, everything changed. All of a sudden, I realized I was a conduit from all the people who had come before me to all those who would come after, beginning with Chip.

I was a cigarette smoker at that time—had been since elementary school days–and it occurred to me that I had "taken-up" smoking because I first; thought it was cool, second, most of my friends were doing it, and third; because I had watched my dad do it, and that fact made it **the** *thing* to do for me. I wanted to be just like him you know. Most of us little boys do that I think.

That *day*, I quit. Four pack-a-day, Winston Cigarettes, nervous habit–gone, because I knew if Chip saw *me* smoke, he might think it was a good thing too.

A parent's influence is far greater than most of us realize. But the same is true for the influence our kids have on us. When Clint was born in May '79, our family was complete and the "uniquely American pursuit of happiness" was underway.

Living in the country there are jobs that your kids are assigned; Hauling trash, picking up limbs, mowing grass, washing cars, and so on. Both our sons spent time riding on the lawnmowers with me beginning when they were just toddlers.

They drove pick-ups around the farm long before they were old enough and could swim and operate motor-boats about as soon as they could walk.

Ever the worker, Chip would finish his "chores" and disappear. Usually, he would get a shovel and create ditches, dams, ponds, and terraces in our yard. He was always fascinated with earth moving and learned to operate machinery as a small child.

Bulldoziers, excavators, backhoes, tractors, if there was a machine close by, Chip would be operating it flawlessly in a very short time. His love for machinery has led him to the world of aviation and it would appear his career will be based on flying with a likely sideline in the heavy equipment world.

That foundation was laid when he was little more than a toddler and Charlotte and I have nurtured that interest and encouraged Chip to see what he could do with it.

Harry Truman was right: He said the best way to advise young people is to figure out what it is they love to do and help them do it!

Chip now holds the MEii–(multi-engine-instrument-instructor) rating which is one step short of the ATP-(Air Transport Pilot) rating, the highest available, and at this writing, he's flying charter out of Atlanta with more than 3,000 hours flight experience and considering an Air Force career.

Naturally, I am very proud of his accomplishments and more than anything, that he has his "head on straight" and appears to be headed into a productive, satisfying, and rewarding career.

Clint loves the outdoors. Pond fishing, river-fishing, turkey hunting, deer hunting, birds, if it has to do with hunting, Clint is the man to know. There are pictures all over our home of Clint as a small boy holding bass that are almost as large if not larger than he is.

Charles M. Williams

When he was barely big enough to see over the steering wheel, he could hook a pan-fishing boat to his Jeep and head off to ponds all over the farm and come back with a "mess" of white perch or bream and occasionally a near-record bass.

Deer season is a special time for Clint. Up well before day and out to his prearranged stand, properly prepared and equipped, he is a knowledgable student of wildlife and has taken numerous trophy deer–their horns and mounted heads adorn the walls of his room along with bass, turkey feet and beards, ducks, and prized shotguns and rifles. Rabbit hounds, bird-dogs, deer-dogs, and retrievers are his forte'. Jack Russell terriers are his sideline!

Likely, the only thing more important to Clint than hunting itself, is his incredible gift for and love of Labrador Retrievers. His patience and skill in training dogs is legendary. His dogs are highly disciplined and respond to his slightest command, knowing exactly what he expects and striving to please their master. He has a gift with animals.

It is a pleasure to watch him work his dogs whether on a rabbit hunt or watching a lab jump out of his boat, swim across a river or a slew, find the duck he shot, and bring him back to the boat. It is amazing to see the relationship between young man and animal.

I realized just how smart Clint was when, after four-years of college, he had never had a class that started before lunch on a Monday nor one that ended after 9:00 p.m. on Thursday. That way, he had Friday, Saturday, Sunday and Monday morning for hunting and fishing. You gotta' admit, that's sharp!

Both boys are a pleasure for Charlotte and me. Chip is a commercial pilot, a Charter Captain for Pat Epps of Epps Aviation in Atlanta. Clint has just completed work on his undergraduate program at Georgia Southern and will continue working on his Masters degree at Georgia College. He is following the same philosphy with the addition of a lake house on Lake Sinclair. Smart Guy!

The very best compliment I can pay to these young men is, as we say in the south, "they've been raised right,. I would hasten to add, "their mamma did a great job!"

However, life is not without problems. Alcohol is out there. So are all the other drugs and sex and many other mind-boggling situations a person can and will be faced with these days. It is different than it was in the 1950s and 1960s and that difference requires a different approach to meeting the challenges as you raise kids today.

Alcohol is an age-old problem with people in my family, as with so many others across the country. I am convinced the problem won't end with this or any other generation. The business is just too profitable. We just have to learn to deal with it on our own terms in our own times.

In my case, dealing with it means abstinance. I don't fault anyone else for partaking if they control themselves, but in my case, I eventually and very slowly learned I was strange enough sober!

Alcohol has an unusual effect on people in my family. Years ago at a family reunion, that's an appointed place and time where lots and lots of people just like me gather to meet folks they don't know and try to remember if they have ever seen any of them before.

It's a time of telling little boys that they "sure look like their momma" (always a universal hit with little boys everywhere) or that they "sure have grown since the last time you saw 'em," (a ploy no kid believes because he or she doesn't want to hear some fat, middle-aged person tell him or her how much they have grown, and besides, the kid has never seen this middle-aged person before, anywhere anytime and, doesn't want to see them again, ever).

What a great time! You can learn a little about the family tree from which you fell and get to know some of the characters your parents may have told you about. Best deal of all, you get to eat what turns out to be some pretty good cookin'!

Grandpa loved alcohol and took advantage of every occasion to imbibe. Family reunions were wonderful opportunities to crawl in a bottle, and it wasn't long before grandpa just disappeared.

Now just imagine, me and a whole bunch of other folks who look, act, and even think a lot like me were hunting grandpa. We eventually found him out behind the barn. Yes, there was an empty quart bottle of Jack Daniels just outside a pig stye (that's a pig pen for them what is uneducated in such thangs):

As we got closer, we saw Grandpa, down on his knees with his left arm wrapped around the neck of a 400 pound sow. That ol' sow was lookin' at him and makin' that familiar grunt, grunt, grunt sound.

Grandpa was looking her straight in the face through his alcohol-saturated eyes and he said, "You know what, (pause) Gertie" (granny's name), "Me and you'se been married for (slurred) Thurrrddddyyy seben years, an' this the first time I ever noted that you had two rows of buttons on your gown!" (Joke. Real names changed to protect the innocent).

We didn't set out to force our sons to stay away from alcohol, although Charlotte and I would both prefer that course.

Instead, what we chose to do was our best to make them aware of the serious consequences of drinking, like drunk driving fatalities, shattered lives, and health problems just to make a short list.

Charles M. Williams

A few hours spent in coordination with a local sheriff and an empty jail cell along with an hour or so of community service with a yard rake are the kinds of first-hand experiences that can help a young man understand the cost of driving under the influence of alcohol.

We don't say "don't drink". We say "here are the potential costs" associated with that activity and ask whether it's worth the potential cost! So far, so good!

It's just our way of accomplishing what Tom Brokaw talked about in his wonderful book, "The Greatest Generation" where he describes people of another era meeting the challenges of their times with the energy, enthusiasm, and the absolute will to overcome any obstacle–financial, physical, mental, or otherwise- to protect the freedoms we enjoy.

We've attacked a serious problem with our own matter-of-fact senses and understanding, and hopefully, we have been effective.

By the way, if you haven't done so already, read Tom Brokaw's books. You'll meet some really amazing people there, people to whom we all owe a great debt of gratitude. Read the books and while you're at it, say a little prayer of thanks for the teachers who patiently taught you to read and the country that made your (and my) education possible in the first place.

Eat Here & Get Gas!

I believe every generation of Americans has within it the same desirable attributes of decisiveness, courage, commitment, and intestinal fortitude among others.

Faced with the similar challenges as those faced by earlier generations, I firmly believe all Americans will work and fight to protect our freedom and our right to pursue happiness, whatever the cost. As Americans, our individual paths may well be different, but our ultimate goals of freedom and independence have and will always be the same. It is that difference, our individuality, that makes America unique in the world.

Considering the fact that we do live in an ever changing world, I am thankful to live in the part of it known as the "Good Old USA," and "Southern by the Grace of God!"

Hafta' sit on my hands

'Got to admit, it's gettin' better, a little better all the time!"
Lenon-McCartney

Nobody can tell the future, except maybe the gypsies with their crystal balls and the palm readers and the guys with robes who walk along the side of the highway with signs proclaiming the end of time.

I don't put a lot of stock there. 'Question is, "Why worry about it?" I have always been a firm believer in the concept that worry doesn't help anything. If you can do something about something, then, as Nike says, "Just Do It!" If there is nothing you can do about a particular thing, then, it's time to move on to something else! What point is there to worrying? Why worry about something totally out of your control?

'Fact is, just as the Bible says, tomorrow will have worries enough of its own. Yesterday is past and cannot be changed. Today is a *gift*; that's why its called the "present!" Take advantage of the opportunities that are here, now, this day, this hour.

As I write these lines, it is an absolutely gorgeous Sunday afternoon in November. The wind is calm. The sun is bright. My work is actually caught up. Tomorrow is a land (as opposed to flying) trip to Covington, Georgia for lunch. I could be spending this afternoon watching football, and, as much as I enjoy waking up now and again to see what the score happens to be, I thought, what a great time to crank up this little laptop, open this project, and put a few thoughts on paper. My Martin porch guitar is right here. I can pick a little, sing a little, write a little, and listen to the lovely sounds of birds and occasional aircraft overhead.

A friend of mine asked me over the phone, "Howyadowin, CHA-rellllzs?" (Another of those pesky little Southern runtogether words we use so often. "How are you today?" might be a more sophisticated, Northern translation. But "Howyadowin" seems to work pretty well in my neck of the woods.

I respond as usual, "I don't know if I could be any better, Paul!" (Paul Eason is a former bank president & friend of mine from Vidalia (Yessir! That *is* where those wonderfully sweet *Vidalia* onions originated and are still grown).

I asked, "Howboutchu" (How about you?)

He said, "Man, I hafta' sit on my hands just to keep from clapping!"

Now, I don't know about you, but I think that is one of the very best answers I have ever gotten! Just picture it! See a guy sitting at his desk. Normal Picture, however, in his mind, things are

Eat Here & Get Gas!

so good and he is sooooo excited that he literally has to *sit on his hands* just to keep from *clapping!*

What an attitude! What a zest for life! My friend Paul exhibits that approach every day and it has carried him quite a distance in his career, family, civic organizations, and every other facet of his life–including three bank conversions within the last few years–buy-outs are rampant in Georgia just now!

Paul is an inspiration and I hope his excitement has been transferred to you in these few lines. We would all do well to adopt his enthusiasm.

You can wait 'till something is better. You can wait till somebody brings you something you think you want. You can wait for a new job, a new house, a new car, a new girlfriend, or for that off-yonder-in-the-future time when you think things are going to be better, but not me.

I'd rather be like my friend Paul and realize that things are just incredibly good now, and they're getting better *all* the time.

Think about it:
I was able to get up this morning!
I could move around!
I was able to eat a good breakfast!
I slept on clean sheets last night!
I had clean, comfortable clothes to wear!
I was surrounded by people who care about me!
My family is healthy!

Charles M. Williams

We have a great home!
Our business is prospering!
We live in Georgia! We live in America!
The holiday season is just ahead.

When you really stop for a moment and think it through, Paul is right: I do hafta' sit on my hands just to keep from clapping! I bet you are in the same boat if you simply stop long enough to look at all you have to be thankful for.

'Fact is, that might be an excellent use of a little of your time *every day!* As my ole'd daddy would remind me, "I felt sorry for myself that I didn't have no shoes till I came up on a man didn't have no feet!" Where exactly are you in terms of the many positive things that are on your side as you read this line! I bet you really need to sit on your hands just to keep from clapping!

Where'd That Come From?

I love these kinds of "sayings" and always wondered what they meant?
Cohen Doudy, barber

Now here's an idea for you: 90 to nothin! Just exactly what does that mean? The odds don't sound too good to start out with, unless of course you're on the 90 side and it's a basketball game. But what exactly does 90 to nothin mean? You've probably heard the expression among Southern folks, "He was goin' 90 to Nothin'" down the "Highway to Hell!"

Now, to me that would mean somebody was moving mighty fast in the wrong direction, but "still and all" (another good Southern colloquialism and doubt if anybody really knows what that one means either) 'fact is that's one of the favorite lines of a local bank president, Joe Taylor uses: "I know you have had loans here in the past and that you did pay them back. *Still and all*, just because you paid them back and were only late on two-thirds of your payments, I can *not* make you this new loan you want!" See how it works? *Still and all,* I'd have to say it works pretty good!

Now, back to the idea of "90 to nothin." You know, it could mean a sudden stop. For example, as Brother Dave told us about Mr. Charles

(Pronounced CHA-rellllz) the Harley rider, and Miss Baby, (his girlfriend, with her leather jacket on backwards to keep the cold out, Charellllz idea). They were riding his Harley motorcycle, she was in the sidecar (like the one Elvis had) and they were going 90 miles an hour when he "come" up behind a slow moving semi-truck. Things was OK till CHA-rellllz read that sign on the back of that truck that said: *"I may be slow, but I'm ahead of you."*

You could just *tell* CHA-rellllz was upset the way he romped down on his Harley and was going 90 miles an hour passin' that truck when he and Miss Baby went head on into the side of the mountain, they was teeth, hair, and eyes *all* over the highway. Spoked wheels spinning, police cars roaring to the scene with fishin poles (eva' body knowed them was radio antennas but they looked like fishin' poles, you know) on the back goin' swish, swish, swish.

According to eyewitnesses-(two little black boys nearby) Mr. CHA-relllz, he was dead, *instantly*, but Miss Baby, she was *ah-ite* 'till me an Junior *turned her head around…"*

That could be one outlandish example of "90 to Nothin" but what does the term mean and why is it still in use even today?

I think it means moving too fast and never stopping to take time to "smell the roses!" I expect

Eat Here & Get Gas!

it is closely related to the term lickety-split, but I won't go anywhere near the origins for that one!

No doubt both of those "speed" related terms are tied somehow to this one: "Flat out runnin'!" 'Now there's a Southern phrase for you. Does that mean running faster on some flat surface, say as opposed to some hilly or unlevel surface? If so, does that mean you might run slower than if on other than flat land or could it be that someone could be both *flat out* on the ground as if had been attacked by a steamroller, and yet, *running* at the same time?

Can you imagine the problems the Japanese, not to mention the rest of the world, encounter attempting to learn English language?

It's further complicated when they are attempting to learn "Southern" English. 'Fact is, we take our own speech patterns absolutely for granted.

I know that you know what it was I said and I am virtually certain that you understood it just exactly as I wrote it and meant for you to comprehend it. You could call that "might-nearly" correct. *"Purt'*-nearly" wouldn't be as accurate as *Might*-nearly, and neither of them would come close to *most*-nearly which is a distance itself from "zackly" as in the term, ass-y-tzack-ly right, which is of course, translated for the uninitiated simply means, *"That's exactly"* as in ass-y-zkly *right* in and of itself. YAWIMME? (Not an indian word, but a contrived, Southern-drawl, shortening of the words in the question: "Are you with me?" See? **Yawimme?** It's right up there with the other famous shortening of the question or term of agreement, depending on the inflection with which it is uttered: **Ah-ite?**

Phonetically, it would be: ah ite'; for the longer, more proper phrase, "will that be *all right* with you, sir, or madam?" if it is a question directed toward a man or a woman, respectively—you figure out the "sir" or "mam" by the head-turn of the speaker as he or she addresses either a male or a female person, or the more contrite: "Ah-ite", pronounced, aaaa-*ite*', if used as a term of agreement:

"Ahite", I kin do 'at! Translated, that means: All right. Yes! I can do that!

Ahite? Yawimme? Know Zackly what I mean?

Here's one other example that I think you'll enjoy. How many times has any good, Southern "mommer" worth her salt given that frisky little admonition to her charges with the very good intention of saying "Behave, or else." I know I've heard it quite a few times, "Now Charles, when you go over to Sarah and Cooper's house today, you be sure you "mind your Ps and Qs! You know she'll tell me if you do something bad!'

Eat Here & Get Gas!

Of course, I knew she would. She did whether I did something bad or not! Miss Sarah was my mother's spy and convenient plant in elementary school, placed there for the sole purpose of watching me to see when, *not if*, I got into something, she made a "B" line—there's another one—wouldn't a B line necessarily *be* crooked? And wouldn't the phrase *"Making a B Line"* seem to indicate the very shortest distance between points "A" and "B" you know, like a straight line. So, where does the phrase "Making a B line"— from which you would logically infer, a really quick, straight, no time wasted—*come* from? Confusing isn't it?

No wonder folks from everywhere else think southerners might all just be a bit *off* the mental mark. I'm beginning to wonder myself, but not for long. I understand perfectly! **Yawimmie?**

The admonition, **"Mind your Ps & Qs"** seems to mean something about being on one's best behavior.

In fact, the concept originated in the pubs of England! In years gone by, English pubs served brew in containers, mugs if you will, that were measured in pints and quarts. When the barkeeper was about to slide a fresh mug down the bar to a waiting patron, to avoid striking pint or a quart container along the way, he sang out, *"Mind your Pints and Quarts, mates"* to all the active patrons along the way.

The phrase, *"pints and quarts"* was progressively shortened over the years to **"Ps and Qs"**.

Thus, the terms that my sainted mother and so many other erudite women of culture in our country use to try and tame their young,

"Mind your Ps & Qs"

is actually derived from the, horror of horrors, pubs of England. Here we call them names like "local bars" and "water gardens" in the north and just plain ol' "juke-joints" in the south.

Hardly the phraseology these prim and proper ladies would select to instruct their young had they but known from whence these phrases had come, but such is the way!

Many of us have indeed gone on to mind Our "Ps and Qs" in the traditional fashion, much to the chagrin of our "mums"!

Confused? Please, don't be. These are just a few of the many words and phrases in use every day in the south. I was born here. I grew up here. I use these phrases frequently and sometimes, when I stop to think about them, I am amazed as well and very proud to be Southern!

Now, I know people from every part of the country have similarly humorous language "things" with which they are so familiar, they don't even *notice* them anymore, but they exist.

Eat Here & Get Gas!

Think about yours! I guarantee you they exist, and with a little imagination, you can have fun with them.

In fact, learning just a bit about these phrases might help us all understand each other a little better, and isn't that what it's all about. I think so!

Ahite? Yawimme? Assyzklyright! Be sure to "Mind your P's & Q's, now, *ya-heah!*

Amazing!

Joy and happiness are both available. Lots of people think they're the same thing.
Dr. Jerry Peele

Every time I have the privilege to speak and play guitar for a group I am certain, nobody in the building has more fun than me.

Getting people to laugh with me and my family and my experiences and at themselves is challenging and very rewarding...fact is, ya'll, it's fun! The thrill of entertaining is the highest of highs for me, and I look forward to every opportunity.

Years ago, as I was creating the thought process for my programs, I made a commitment to close every program with the beautiful old gospel hymn, "Amazing Grace". I can't sing it like Elvis or any of the many great voices, but, remember, I don't *have* to. All I have to do is sing it to the best of my abilities, and that's what I do. It's what I encourage everyone to do. Whether it's singing a song, writing a sentence, painting a room or running a company, your best *is* good enough!

I have performed for diverse groups; from politicians to preachers; to bank groups and business organizations, all across the U.S. I have yet to find a group that did not respond positively to this beloved hymn. In fact, somehow, someway, I believe it is a part of what I was put here to do.

My youngest son was in Sunday School one morning and the teacher told him: "We's all put here to serve *others!* Clint responded with a question: "What'uz them *others* put here for? 'Sorry, 'couldn't resist that one!

I think a bit of explanation is in order. I believe we are all here for one purpose and that is to serve others. Some people do it by providing healthcare and I deeply admire anyone who has the gift of care-giving. Others serve through providing financial advice and assistance. Some serve in the military, in police operations, and thousands of other ways, but the end result is that we are all here to serve the needs of other people. We keep score by how well we actually accomplish that task and usually, the score card is gauged by monetary gain, houses, cars, bank accounts, etc.

Preachers seem to have the most difficult job because the *best* ones do the *most* work, and according to the typical American scorecard measurement, they achieve the least, from a material perspective.

In my business, the scorecard rewards have been phenomenal and improving annually. But by the truest measure, I believe, thanks to my great friends Pastors David Smith and Jerry Peele, I am spreading just a bit of happiness *and joy* among my audiences. That's a big plus for me. That's why I work as hard as I do to make my audiences as happy and excited as I am.

"Happiness" is available practically anywhere: The stock market when you've had a gain; a new job with a better salary or better working conditions; good news that your physical exam didn't turn up any problem; a good, deep down belly laugh when you hear something funny! All these and literally thousands of other things can make us happy (or sad as the case may be). However, "Joy" is different.

Joy isn't something you can get from a joke or a good run of luck in business, your family, your marriage, or any other place but one.

Friends, in my best Jimmy Swaggert (You know, I used to want to be either a Televangelist or a Politician till I discovered I didn't have the sex drive for either one!) televangelist voice, that place is a belief in the greater power of the God who created the very universe in which we all exist.

Believing in His power which is so much greater than any or all of us, puts things in proper perspective and gives us a sense of orientation unavailable through any other means.

From that perspective, you can see that our days are numbered and our longest lives are but a short time in the continuum. It makes you realize that every one of us has a purpose. Many never find it. That's bad. Many never look and that's worse. Fact is, it's there all the same.

I believe our purpose is summed up in a simple formula outlined in the acronym for the word J-O-Y. First, <u>J</u>esus, the God of the universe, the creator of all things, you and me included. Second, <u>O</u>ther people and their needs second. <u>Y</u>ourself and your needs would be last in the correct happiness formula.

You can achieve happiness in many ways but "joy" comes in just one. I'd like to challenge and encourage you to pursue both happiness and joy all your days. It is your right. It is your privilege. It is the only true path and it is available to every human being…all the time!

If not now, When?

Nothing in the world is more common than unsuccessful men with talent.
Calvin Coolidge

I was most fortunate to be the youngest child in my family, eight years younger than my sister, Pat, and four years younger than my brother, Verne.

Pat married a fine man from Chicago, *(imagine that)*, and she and Keith, Dr. Keith Mathews, have raised two outstanding daughters, Stephanie, an elementary school teacher in Tampa, and Laura, an International Business lady *(person)* who lives in Virginia.

The Mathews live in Bradenton, Florida *(imagine that too)* and are very successful and happily married people.

Pat drives me insane by absolutely never forgetting birthdays, anniversaries, the day we got the dog, new car days, it is endless, and it is uniquely, Pat.

There is no more loving person in the world. I talk about her quite a bit and love to tell audiences that: "When my sister moved to Florida, the I.Q. average went up in both states!"

She is the person who has encouraged me more than anyone. That trip she arranged for me to see Dave Gardner, live, in Daytona struck home. I love Pat and her family dearly.

Recently, Pat was diagnosed with breast cancer. As you would readily imagine, everyone was very down and depressed about it...with the exception my sister PAT. Indeed not, she simply took the surgery, the chemo-therapy and radiation, endured every difficulty and hardship and never lost a step at calling and sending cards and doing just exactly like Pat has always done...giving herself for others. In fact, the treatments have opened up a whole new world for her as she is well acquainted with and in close personal contact with a new set of friends, all of whom and their families are going through the same terrible struggle.

The world would be better if there were more Pat Mathews and Irene Chances around, no question about it. I'm most fortunate to claim both as close kin!

My brother Verne had more talent than any one person I have met in this world, bar none. He created pen and ink artwork that is just beautiful. The detail is incredible and beyond my imagination. He spent months sketching and inking drawings of historic buildings around our hometown such as the churches and the old train depot. No doubt these treasures will always be around as a tribute to his enormous talents long after most of us are gone and forgotten.

Eat Here & Get Gas!

Verne's talents as a musician were equally tremendous. He could play guitar in the Chet Atkins/Merle Travis finger-style and he was awesome. His gift was recognized by everyone fortunate enough to have heard him play. I always believed his pickin' was as good as any player anywhere in the country.

On top of that, he had a beautiful harmony voice. I just knew he and I would combine our talents to make ourselves a name and a good living in the entertainment business. We worked together for several years in that direction. There was just one two-headed obstacle to that wonderful life we both thought about and talked about through the years. It was those age-old problems called drugs and alcohol.

"Aw, man, a little pot won't hurt you," I heard him say hundreds of times. "I don't drink too much! Why don't you just leave me alone and let me mind my own business? You mind yours!"

Then, in August 1994, a terrible accident destroyed those dreams as he became a C-4 quadrapelegic with no use of his body from the neck down. None.

It was just a simple fall. Not an automobile accident though he had survived several of those. Nothing dramatic. Nothing gruesome. The incident itself was totally simple, yet devastating and life-altering.

Charles M. Williams

He had a few drinks, sat down in a chair on his front porch and fell asleep. He woke up in the early morning hours, August 14th, stood up, lost his balance and fell over a three foot porch rail. He dropped three feet straight down on the back of his head, forever crushing his spinal column at the forth cervical vertebra.

"It is a *complete* injury" the doctors at Shepard Spinal Clinic said. We eventually learned that means *absolute and never healing.*

He's endured breathing machines, surgeries, diapers, lung suctions, and twenty-four hour nursing care since that day, eight years and slowly counting.

His time is measured now between infections, blockages, and other health problems. There is no movement beyond the shoulders. There will be none. He was 47 at the time of the accident, the very prime of life. He could survive for decades.

Alcohol. "Aw', it won't hurt you, man!" To consider drinking it and taking the associated risks is beyond my comprehension. There has never been and *never will be* a person born who can handle it. In the end, it *always* wins.

Every time! You lose! The potential costs are totally disproportionate to any rewards! In Verne's case we will continue to miss the delightful opportunity to enjoy both the art and musical talents of one truly gifted individual. When it comes to alcohol and drugs the only choice is abstinence. None again. Period.

The key to success in this life is not talent. That's certainly important and it helps, but it isn't the key. Verne certainly had that. And it isn't education either, he held a Masters Degree in Vocational Education. There are thousands of educated derelicts. The only true keys are Joy and dogged persistence. Establish a goal. Write it down, and pursue it with all your energy, strength, and enthusiasm. Avoid the age-old pitfalls!

Recognize and avoid the false shackles and the artificial crutches. They are just empty promises that, in the end, *deny* happiness and joy. They are like a thief in the night. Like an unwelcome guest who doesn't leave until you take control and throw him out. Verne, unfortunately, never got the message. He will steadfastly argue in favor of pot and beer even to this day.

Almost every time I end a speaking program, I challenge the audience with this thought: "Don't drink. Don't smoke. Don't use tobacco *(unless it's for a bee sting)*; Don't run around on your spouse. Eat the right foods. Don't eat too much. Exercise! Go to church. Fact is, following these rules may not make your life a bit longer, *but it'll shore seem like it!*

Charles M. Williams

"When I got up this morning, I really did hafta' to sit on my hands…just to keep from clapping!" In fact, it is very hard to type in this condition.

Steps to Happiness Everybody Knows:

You can't be all things to all people.
You can't do all things at once
You can't do all things equally well.
You can't do all things better than everyone else.
Your humanity is showing just like everyone else's.
So:
You have to find out who you are, and be that.
You have to decide what comes first, and do that.
You have to discover your strengths, and use them.
You have to learn not to compete with others,
Because no one else is in the contest of *being you*.

Then:
You will have learned to accept your own uniqueness.

Eat Here & Get Gas!

You will have learned to set priorities and make decisions.
You will have learned to live with your limitations.
You will have learned to give yourself the respect that is due.

And you'll be a most vital mortal.
Dare To Believe:
That you are a wonderful, unique person.
That you are a once-in-all-history event.
That it's more than a right, it's your duty, to be who you are.
That life is not a problem to solve, but a gift to cherish.
And you'll be able to stay one up on what used to get you down.

- Author Unknown

You really don't need drugs or alcohol. None of us do!

Thanks for reading this. It is my sincere hope you've enjoyed reading it just half as much as I have writing it!

$4,250.00 Turkey

There is no greater calling than being a dad!
Vernon Williams

It was springtime, Spring Strut, Fall Rut, in hunting language. I suppose fish bite better in certain times too, for example, white perch seem to bed up in ponds in the early spring. There is so much to know about hunting and fishing if you are going to be successful at it!

Somehow I missed most of that in my earliest days. I was always interested in machines, cars, trucks, "glass-pack" mufflers...mag wheels. I loved guns and owned several. In fact, I was a cracker-jack shot with a twenty two rifle...take out a turtle half way across a pond...and popping a target dead on was no problem. However, my dad didn't hunt, likely due to his painful left leg, and, consequently, golf, outdoor activities, and particularly hunting, were never encouraged in my home. I think I might have missed something along there somewhere but more than made up for it in my lifelong love of machinery.

That love has been 100 percent transferred to my oldest son. Chip loves flying. Aerobatic flying is his deepest love. Hammer-head stalls, rolls, loops, spins, Immelman turns, likely one of these days the very aggressive Lumchevak maneuver...you name it, Chip loves flying practically any aircraft. Although his "day Job" is flying as the Captain of a Beechcraft King Air charter plane and the executive twin-engined Lear-jet, he flies a Beechcraft Aerobatic Bonanza painted a shiny red-white and blue with stars and smoke at airshows. He is at the top of his game when it's time to perform for an audience. (Well, maybe when he has the opportunity to take his mom or his dad up to show them what it feels like to be in the plane WHILE he is Practicing...that might even be better...but for the most part, flying any type of aircraft is sheer joy to Chip). Like his ole' man, he can shoot with accuracy. He can fish with patience, and he can hunt well enough to eat if he has to but his passion is machines, especially flying machines. Getting a type rating in a twin engine jet is pure joy for him. Somehow I can appreciate that fact.

Clint, on the other hand, loves hunting and fishing with every bit as much pure passion. Fortunately, his first cousin is an avid and experienced hunter who has unselfishly shared his experiences with Clint since his earliest boyhood days. Hunter safety courses and the practiced hand of his mentor, Jim Green and his cousin, Ron Walker, plus the watchful and experienced eyes of

Eat Here & Get Gas!

the Walker family and their hunting and fishing paradise on the Ocmulgee River in Telfair County have created a serious and successful hunter ole' Clint.

Deer heads and antlers abound in our house. Photos of aircraft and models are everywhere. There are largemouth bass mounts on the walls, hunting supply catalogs on every table, deer scent bottles, fish hooks, trot lines, nets, rods, reels, shotguns, powerful rifles, scopes…knives, camouflage clothing, snake boots…oh what a long and expensive list…and that's just inside the house. Practically anytime you come inside you'll find a TV playing with no one in sight, and it will usually be the Outdoor Channel! Step outside and you'll find Toyota four-wheel drive pickups, "john" or "crappie" style or flatwater fishin' boats, 50 HP motors, every kind of rod, reel, pole, pole holder, pistol, and plug you can dream up. Ahh, the joy of raising boys!

This year, Clint invited me to accompany him on his absolute favorite art in the business of hunting wild game and that is Turkey hunting. Literally for months before the season comes in, he is busy. There are areas to clear. There is food to put out. There are signs to watch. There are guns to prepare. Shells to acquire, calls to buy and practice and perfect. Camo to buy and fit and try.

Charles M. Williams

Without experiencing the process first hand, it is difficult to believe what serious turkey hunters go through to prepare to hunt this most challenging and dubious bird.

Studying the habitat and habits of a turkey is a science in and of itself. The fact that a turkey will "roost" in a certain area say as opposed to another certain area is amazing. How serious hunters can determine which is which is even more amazing. The fact that they can, with experience, not only do that but also with some precision, estimate when and where these very wary birds will "fly down" and approximate "when" that will occur is nothing less than natural science.

To make myself eligible to go on a turkey hunt with a hunter of Clint's caliber there were days of training. First off, there was the gear question. Did I have an appropriate shotgun? Of course not! None, no not one of the multiple Browning, Remington, or Benelli arms that Clint had received as Christmas presents over the years was precisely right for me for this turkey hunt. Indeed, this one needed to be the famed Black Eagle from Benelli, a wonderfully camouflaged 12 guage automatic that will accept all the different types of shotgun shells, up to and including the 3 and ½ inch Magnum variety…an enormously powerful round that adds that certain distance to your "kill" zone. That's important when it is a wild turkey you are pursuing. Put $1,200 on your shopping list if you are keeping tabs here, and go ahead and multiply by two since I get to buy for both of us! Of course these same wonderful shotguns can be used for dove hunting, duck hunting, and practically any other variety. Even better, Clint may be able to find a use for them if I happen not to be along at the time. What an excellent idea!

Then of course, there are the authorized and licensed Browning socks, underwear, camo T-shirts, and headnets (one can never underestimate the marvelous sense of sight and sound possessed by every turkey, let alone the really wise old birds. Put $300 into the till for those few items and don't forget to multiply.

Naturally, there are the shells and they are cheaper buy the case and at the right time of the year, there are special bargains to be had: add another $100 just for good measure.

Next come boots. Remember, it is springtime in central Georgia. The weather is beautiful and warming up. Every living creature is delighted about the prospect of good weather and practically all of them are out and about in this season, especially the famed Diamond Back rattlesnake which is common in this area. Serious snake boots are a must. Just about knee high is best, and totally camouflaged is imperative. There is a specific brand name that is the preference of the serious hunters. It is called the Outback and you can understand these very valuable and reasonably comfortable boots are sold for the bargain price of just $100 per leg! Put another $400 in the till.

One other group that is out in force as nature brings springtime to the woods and creek basins of Georgia is the mosquito. No, your net is not for mosquito protection. It only serves to camouflage your face to the eye of the turkey. Without proper mosquito protection, you will be carried away long before any turkey will come anywhere near your position. Plus, you cannot "slap" a mosquito…regardless of the circumstances. A turkey will hear that from several acres away and avoid you and your area like the plague.

Add at least $50 for Mosquito sprays and various concoctions that will keep them away without alerting the turkey. In fact, there is a new device out now that really works…a portable propane, pocket device that clears an area with you in the center. You just hope it doesn't run out of gas before you take your bird! Don't forget to double your prices here!

Hats are an absolute must in this business. The right camouflage hat is invaluable and literally takes months and even years to properly break in. It can have the name of your favorite car dealer, builder's supply or parts store sewn or inked on it…and if it does, it's usually Free…best kind! No

Eat Here & Get Gas!

add on here if you are keeping tabs. However, mine does have the Ford Motor Company logo on it, just for good measure. Came from one of my very favorite customers, Riverside Ford in Macon! Add $12.00!

Then there is the all important vest. Naturally it must be camouflage. It must have secret compartments to quietly and adequately store and carry all your calls, sprays, shells, and other gear. It should have a built in seat cushion for you to sit down on as you wait for your bird. The best ones even have a seat back you can lean on for support. $200 for one of these wonderful devices is just a deal. Put another $200 in the till.

Your camouflage overalls are the mainstay for the program. Get 'em loose and comfortable with loads of pockets. No telling what you'll need when you get there, you know, like emergency toilet paper...it is early morning you know and sometimes the spirit can move you at just the wrong time...Add another $150 for the overalls. The paper is N/C!

Finally, the right shirt is another imperative. If it doesn't say Browning, or NWTF (National Wild Turkey Federation) sponsored, why, then, it's just a common shirt and hardly worth wearing. Camouflage of course and only another $100. Oh, but you do look good!

Then it's time to learn to imitate the sounds a turkey might make and respond to. Of course, you can buy cheap calls or you can buy the handmade, forever, beautifully, one of a kind, four kinds of specialty wood, did I mention hand made, beauties made by this ingenious old timer who knows more about turkeys than Noah...and of course makes the absolute best turkey call known to man...a collector's item one day to be sure...and you only add another $85 for that (plus a $20 camo case to hook on your belt...and you're ready to start the training.

Up and at 'em at 5:15 AM, headed out in all your new, beautiful, camo gear, boots, shotgun, vest...headed to the spot where your guide, in this case Ole' Clint, has "roosted" a bird the day before. Quietly, swiftly, not stepping on twigs that will crackle and leaves that will rattle, hardly breathing and never breathing hard, through the darkness of the early morning woods, always aware of how truly valuable your camouflaged, knee high snake boots really are. The walk can be long and fast. Glasses tend to fog from the body heat and your vision gets blurred. Your ears tightly tuned and listening for the sound of a gobbler. The call of an owl in the distance excites the old bird and he gobbles in the distance. You freeze and try to determine exactly where, which direction, and how far you are from the bird. Moving swiftly ever closer, quietly, approaching just the spot from which to lean against a tree and

Eat Here & Get Gas!

position yourself in the likely direction you expect the gobbler to approach, it is a challenge!

Mosquito spray everywhere, propane unit quietly ablaze to ward off things that bite, trying to be still, trying not to breath loudly, trying to reinstate blood to the left hip and leg which have both grown numb from the tight restriction on movement, it is difficult.

Just then, ole' Clint uses his experience and a $50 store-bought call to accurately portray the sound of a very sexy hen. Now you have to think about this just a moment: During the mating season or the "Spring Strut", a Gobbler or male turkey, is generally surrounded by adoring hens just vying for his attention. For a hunter to be able to lure him away from his harem the sounds he has to create have to be so appealing, so compelling, and so overpowering, that he will find it irresistible! He'll follow his emotions instead of his brain and somewhat cautiously seek out the source of this siren sound!

You can imagine that any movement, however slight will alert the wiry bird and cause him to immediately disappear into the woods once again. A mosquito slap, the twitch of an eye, the movement of a shotgun, the glare off glasses…just the slightest sign and it's over.

Ole' Clint is a young master! His coaching, scouting, calling, purchasing, outfitting, leadership, and natural abilities brought us to this point. Here we were, listening to a turkey gobble in the wild, responding to his skillful calls. Listening, barely breathing, motionless, and excited, we sat, watching for any movement, any sign of the gobbler.

Then, about fifty five yards out, there he was, slightly to the left of our anticipated target range, and moving from our left to our right. When his head went behind a pine tree, I moved my shotgun to the right anticipating his head emerging from behind the tree. My guess was on the money. The gobbler didn't see me move and I was lined up perfectly when his head appeared on the right side of the tree.

I squeezed off one magnum round from that distance and managed to take my first ever gobbler. It was a perfect shot! The bird fell!

Clint sailed over my left shoulder running. He yelled, "Good Shot, Good, Shot, you got him!" He grabbed the flapping wings of what would turn out to be one of the largest, oldest gobblers ever taken on our farm. The spurs were an inch and ¼. The beard was eleven inches, and he weighed 21 pounds. What a trophy! What an experience. What a memory.

Usually, a father teaches his son to hunt, fish, ride a bike and things like that. In this case, the son was the teacher and what a teacher he was. Some experiences are just too good for words but I can just imagine years from now Ole' Clint will tell his children and grandchildren about taking their Grand or great-grandad on his very first turkey hunt. In fact, he can show them the bird himself. Of course I had him mounted. That was the other $600 in this $4,240 turkey hunt!

Charlotte was so pleased when I put that beautiful, expensive, fierce looking turkey in our living room. Ahhh, but what a memory! I gotta tell you, it cost a lot but it was absolutely worth it!

Summary

I hope you've gotten' an idea or two and a smile or two from this project.
CMW

This is a short book. It has a few good ideas and it has been fun to work on. As I begin to think about an end, I believe the effort has helped me understand myself just a bit better. My hope is that as my reader, you too have been affected positively! What purpose has there been to a life that has not made another's life brighter by contact?

What I have tried to say is pretty simple: Treat others as you would like to be treated. That's Biblical. That is wisdom tried and true through all the ages. It's what we should all strive for even though very few of us ever achieve it. Mr. Stuckey did. My dad did. Judge George Hearn did! All of the most successful people I have had the pleasure to have known or even read about were those who gave of themselves to make life better for others. Politicians make the headlines, the statues, and the history books but it's the rest of us who live our lives in smaller ways that most powerfully affect those about us.

How you treat your spouse, how you raise your children, how you either encourage or discourage

Charles M. Williams

every single person you meet has a profound effect on those people…and just as importantly, YOU. The real idea behind writing these thoughts has been to help me and you take a good look at us! Are we lifters or leaners? Do we brighten a room more by entering…*or leaving!* Are people glad you came to the event at hand…or do they wonder why you are here! Are you contributing to the lives of those around you or are you taking away. *What do you choose?*

About the Author

Crazy and proud of it!

Charles Williams is a product of the rural south. He has a delightful sense of humor, a heavy helping of talent, and a depth of energy and enthusiasm that is contagious everywhere he goes.

Charles grew up selling Fords. His dad, Vernon, was the local Ford dealer and selling and making sure friends and customers always got more than they expected has been a standard every day of his life.

Charles didn't listen to those people who told him: ***"It ain't never been done that way before"*** and ***"That won't work."*** Instead, he parted with tradition, created his own business, *an advertising agency in, of all places, Chauncey, Georgia,* and has become very successful as a businessman, a sought after speaker, a finger-style guitar picker, and southern style storyteller. Charles Williams loves to help people laugh! Even better, everybody has a front row seat at his performances.

Williams is a graduate of the University of Georgia, a commercial and instrument rated pilot, an AOPA member, and a former Infantry Officer. Most of all he is a loving father, a dedicated husband, and Christian businessman with a quick wit and a storehouse of characters, impersonations, songs, inspiration and enthusiasm. Get to know Charles through this book! Get him to come to your next event if you want to encourage and delight your groups or audiences!

"This Man really is Crazy…and You'll be Delighted!"